The Reagan Vision

*How You Can Revive
the Reagan Revolution*

GOLDWATER
INSTITUTE

in defense of liberty

Goldwater Institute
500 East Coronado Road
Phoenix, AZ 85004
(602) 462-5000
goldwaterinstitute.org

Library of Congress Control Number: 2004113233

ISBN 0-9761499-0-7

Design by Pagés/BBDO
Dominican Republic

Printed in the Dominican Republic
Editora Centenario, S.A.
Santo Domingo, September 2004

Contents

Authors' Note

We stood in a line that would take us to the Rotunda, the hallowed hall at the heart of the U.S. Capitol where the body of Ronald Wilson Reagan lay in state.

As we looked at our watches, ticking past 1 a.m. on June 10, 2004, we had no idea how long we would be standing in the still summer air. "It's expected to be five and a half hours from this point," one guard told us. With a sigh and shrug, we geared up for a long night.

We knew it would be worth it. We weren't going to miss a chance to pay respects to our favorite American hero. And anyway, the occasion was bringing back personal memories of another shared experience – another all-nighter inspired by the Gipper.

A year a half earlier, when Dan was living in Phoenix and Brad was making a brief weekend visit, we drove through the night to visit the Reagan Library in Simi Valley, California. It was during that road trip that we developed the concept for this book.

Sure, already much has been written about our 40th President: memoirs from his close advisors, detailed biographies from historians, and tributes from others whose personal involvement with Reagan had taught them important life lessons. But these books focused on the past, and as we sped through the moonlit desert toward California, our thoughts were about the future.

Now it's true that we're both decidedly younger than just about everyone else who has written about Reagan. One of your authors remembers the assassination attempt on Reagan as the first news story he watched on TV (at age three and a half). The other, a few years older, traces his earliest news memories (excluding New York Yankee Bucky Dent's homer to beat the rival Boston Red Sox in 1978) to the Iranian hostage crisis that plagued President Carter and made Reagan's election more likely. So you aren't going to get new, inside revelations from the two of us.

But we do have something to contribute as representatives of a younger generation that grew up touched by the ideas and example of Ronald Reagan. Sometime in the not too distant future, the task of preserving the "shining city" will fall to our peers, and then to those who are still younger. As we made that drive out to Simi Valley, we began thinking that there *must* be audience for a book that would discuss the continuing relevance of Reagan's ideas – a book that would try to rally more people to the task of achieving the unfinished goals of the Reagan Revolution.

Over the intervening months, we took a leap of faith and drafted this volume that's in your hands now.

Standing in that line to the Rotunda in the early hours of June 10, 2004 – amid Americans from all walks of life, who had traveled far and wide for a chance to salute Ronald Reagan – we believed our initial hunch had been vindicated. Let us briefly describe the scene.

The line snaked back and forth as though a roller-coaster would be waiting at its end. People shuffled through the line quietly, perhaps out of respect for the solemn occasion or maybe from pure fatigue. There were parents holding the hands of yawning children and whispering to them, "Someday, you will tell *your* grandkids that you saw President Reagan lying in state." We saw an older blind man, using his walking stick to find his way up the Capitol steps, to participate in a ritual he couldn't appreciate with eyes – only with his heart. We heard the stories of out-of-towners who had gone to impressive lengths for their two minutes in the Rotunda. Their voices communicated that they knew their efforts were a bit crazy, but also, that this was the point. Just as you might do in a new romance, they were letting a completely selfless gesture – *I did this for you* – communicate a deep affection and heartfelt sense of gratitude.

We sincerely hope that this book proves useful to those who have mourned the loss of Ronald Reagan, and who would like to see our country return to those principles he espoused.

Our aim is to help sustain and develop the very valuable conversation that emerged after his death. What can we learn from Reagan's incredible career? How can his ideas and his tactics be applied to the problems we face as a country today? And on a more personal level, what can each of us do to play a part in this revival of the Reagan Revolution?

Of course, we don't presume to speak for Reagan. As often as possible, we let Reagan speak for himself, by drawing upon his vast archive of speeches, letters, and commentaries. We do our best to use these guideposts to chart a course for achieving Reaganite goals in the years to come.

The Reagan Vision is divided into four sections. Chapter 1 explains what everyone should know about the Reagan

Revolution and the events that have given conservatives this moment of opportunity. Chapter 2 examines today's domestic policy challenges in light of the main themes of Reagan's political thought. Chapter 3 addresses how Reagan's vision of foreign affairs applies more than ever today. And Chapter 4 is about how the ultimate success of the Reagan Revolution depends on you.

Throughout the text, we have included numerous quotes from Reagan that highlight his key ideas. For those who want to read Reagan unfiltered, we also include an appendix with several of Reagan's most important speeches. And if you would like to join this conversation further, please visit the ReaganVision.com Web site that we have developed as a resource to complement this book.

Before we close, we should acknowledge our great appreciation for all the family and friends who have been so supportive of this project and the work that led to it. We expect you know who you are, and you will forgive us for avoiding a lengthy list here. We are also indebted to all the kindred spirits in the freedom movement, especially those who were working for these ideas when the outlook was much more pessimistic. In that number, of course, we include Ronald Reagan and his wife, Nancy, to whom this book is dedicated.

Forward

By Darcy A. Olsen, CEO & President, Goldwater Institute

It was 1964 when Barry Goldwater recalled to the nation the fundamental purpose of the Republican Party, saying, "We must, and we shall, return to proven ways—not because they are old, but because they are true. We must, and we shall, set the tide running again in the cause of freedom." Forty years later, the same compelling responsibility to advance the cause of freedom rests on today's generation.

The Goldwater Institute is honored to present this volume by two young men who have responded to Goldwater's call, brothers Brad Lips and Dan Lips. *The Reagan Vision* contains ten ideas for each of us to advance freedom in our age, and is a standing reminder that adherence to principle brings success.

Historians trace the roots of the Reagan years to Goldwater's presidential campaign, when Republican principles were rekindled. Three days after the 1964 election, *The Wall Street Journal* editorialized that "there is a deep significance in the revealing statistic that six of every ten voters agreed with the central thesis of Mr. Goldwater's philosophy—namely, that the power of the Federal

Government should be trimmed. Here, then, is a contribution from Barry Goldwater ... what the people heard an honest man say made an impression that could linger long after the man himself has been dismissed. There have been other times in politics when this proved portentous."

And so it did. Ronald Reagan's landslide presidential victory put many Goldwater principles into practice. With the guiding philosophy that "Government is not a solution to our problem, government is the problem," Reagan reduced the income tax from a high of 70 percent to 28 percent and helped hold inflation under 4 percent, leading to the country's longest peacetime economic expansion.

Yet, one need only look to the first four years of this century to observe that fundamental American principles are too infrequently translated into action. Federal spending has risen 30 percent, and recent expansions into health care, education and intimate matters like marriage counseling cause one to wonder whether there are any areas of American life that escape the federal government's purview.

And yet, this is a hopeful time. We need not wait, nor should we, for revolution from the political establishment. As Nancy Reagan said, "Barry started a crusade and handed the torch to Ronnie." That torch, now, is ours to carry. If each of us who believes in the cause of freedom will commit to entering the race, meeting challenges with action rather than apathy, freedom's light will grow.

In Reagan's words, "Let us go forth with good cheer and stout hearts—happy warriors out to seize back a country and a world to freedom."

Chapter 1

The Reagan Revolution

A hush fell over the room as the 53 year-old former actor walked toward the podium at its front. Any nerves that he might have felt were hidden by a brisk stride and comfortable smile, visible manifestations of a confidence that had been nurtured over many years. Even with his fame diminished from his heights as a leading Hollywood star in the 1940s, Ronald Reagan never questioned his ability to communicate his message to an audience. Especially not this message. Especially not in front of this audience.

For more than ten years, Reagan had been talking about free enterprise in front of large groups as a spokesman for General Electric. Crisscrossing the country to give these talks and listen to the questions and concerns of everyday Americans, Reagan had evolved from a New Deal Democrat to a staunch conservative. He had seen daily evidence of the contributions of the private sector, and the ways in which government had become a burden, rather than a help, to individuals. All this firmed his convictions about the merits of capitalism and dangers of big government.

Also, like few in his generation, Reagan understood the communist threat from first-hand experience. He had been president of the Screen Actors Guild at a time when U.S. communists had infiltrated the unions, incited riots, and issued death threats to Reagan and other labor leaders in an attempt to take over the film industry. In the intervening years, he had observed in the actions of the Soviet Union the same duplicity and lust for power he saw in those labor battles.

Now, as the co-chair of the Goldwater campaign in California, he stood before a friendly audience that had gathered to see him give a speech expressing his political views. Several Republican donors had arranged to record the speech and have it broadcast nationally, hoping to revive Barry Goldwater's chances in the approaching presidential election.

At the podium, waiting for the signal to begin, Reagan thumbed through the index cards that held his notes for this speech. To Reagan, the speech was not new: He had been delivering versions of it for months. But to much of the television audience it would reach, the speech was unlike anything they had ever heard. Ronald Reagan's political career would be born with this speech, and it's fair to say that address truly gave new life to American conservativism.

Reagan's speech was titled "A Time for Choosing." In its details, Reagan presented the fundamental questions that Goldwater had been asking in his campaign. Would the country halt the creep toward socialism in its domestic policies? In foreign affairs, would the United States confront the growing imperialist ambitions of the Soviet Union?

But the remarkable aspect of Reagan's speech was how it wrapped these issues into a larger moral vision of America as the keeper of the world's highest ideals: human dignity and individual liberty.

You and I have a rendezvous with destiny. We will preserve for our children this, the last best hope of man on Earth, or we will sentence them to take the last step into a thousand years of darkness.

This was the choice Americans faced. Would the United States set its sights upward toward "the ultimate in individual freedom consistent with law and order" or would it acquiesce to a trend downward toward "the ant-heap of totalitarianism"?

● ● ●

The United States emerged from World War II as the world's pre-eminent military and economic power – and as its lone beacon of freedom. Oceans had kept the American homeland safe from the horrors of World War II. The U.S. economy revived from the hardships of depression and wartime scarcities. Reflecting the benevolence of its people, the U.S. government rebuilt devastated Europe through the Marshall Plan and trade, and helped transform vanquished Germany and Japan into functioning democracies.

But disturbing trends had emerged in the years leading up to 1964. In international affairs, the Soviet Union had tested American resolve and found it wanting. Eastern Europe was bound by Soviet puppet strings immediately following World War II, and President Dwight D. Eisenhower chose not to intervene in Hungary when the Soviet-backed communist government brutally put down a popular uprising in 1956. China fell to communist revolutionaries in 1950, and the United States fought to a stalemate in Korea, allowing communism to remain intact in the north. In the Western hemisphere, Castro's revolution of 1959 put a communist state just 90 miles from Florida. In August 1961, Moscow ordered the construction of the Berlin Wall to end East Germany's access to the freedoms of West Berlin.

President John F. Kennedy had stood up to Soviet Premier Nikita Khrushchev in 1962's Cuban Missile Crisis, but his ultimatums were accompanied by concessions. The United States withdrew military assets from Turkey, and Soviet troops remained in Cuba. Khrushchev's prediction of the inevitability of communism sweeping the earth – "Whether you like it our not, history is on our side. We will bury you." – did not seem unreasonable. After all, even Great Britain had nationalized its major industries, and for all the economic prosperity enjoyed by the United States, the intellectual consensus of the day advocated greater government involvement in the daily lives of citizens.

Certainly this was the view of the incumbent President Lyndon Johnson, who had come of age during President Franklin Roosevelt's New Deal and who championed a vast expansion of power in the federal government to achieve what he termed "the Great Society." In his speech at the 1964 Democratic National Convention, Johnson listed a series of goals: medical care for older citizens, stable prices, decent incomes, decent homes and neighborhoods, good educations, jobs for anyone willing, a reduction of poverty, and on and on.

No one would disagree that these outcomes are desirable. What needed to be challenged, however, was Johnson's assumption that the federal government was the appropriate means for realizing them.

Barry Goldwater earned the responsibility for making the case against Johnson's big government liberalism when he won a bitter nomination fight for Republican Party's presidential ticket. A sharp-jawed businessman, Air Force pilot in World War II, and then U.S. senator from Arizona, Goldwater was a no-nonsense conservative amid a Republican Party that was then dominated by status-quo liberals. Goldwater promised to offer the country "a choice – not an echo." He asserted that encroaching government had to be tamed in order to protect individual liberties and to preserve the economic freedom that had been the engine for America's rise. American greatness had been built by free people, who pursued their own interests and who, by and large, offered help to neighbors in need without deferring to distant bureaucrats.

Where most campaigns cater to groups of Americans by promising them government favors, Goldwater did the opposite. He told Iowans that he would end farm subsidies. He took heat in Tennessee for suggesting that its government boondoggle, the Tennessee Valley Authority, be privatized. He campaigned in the manner suggested in his 1960 book, *The Conscience of a Conservative*, where he asserted the need for politicians who will proclaim:

> *I have little interest in streamlining government or in making it more efficient for I mean to reduce its size. I do not undertake to promote welfare, for I propose to extend freedom. My aim is not to pass laws, but to repeal them. It is not to inaugurate new programs, but to cancel old ones that do violence to the Constitution, or that have failed in their purpose, or that impose on the people an unwarranted financial burden. I will not attempt to discover whether legislation is 'needed' before I have first determined whether it is constitutionally permissible. And if I should later be attacked for neglecting my constituents' 'interests,' I shall reply that I was informed their main interest is liberty and that in that cause I am doing the very best I can.[1]*

---

[1] Goldwater, *The Conscience of a Conservative*, Young Americans for Freedom, Inc., 1970 reprint, pp. 30-31.

Goldwater's adherence to conservative principles caused him to be branded an extremist by an unsympathetic media. Goldwater used his 1964 convention speech to accept that label on his own terms – "Extremism in the defense of liberty is no vice... moderation in the pursuit of justice is no virtue." – and to remind Americans of their country's moral purpose: "The good Lord raised this mighty Republic to be a home for the brave and to flourish as the land of the free – not to stagnate in the swampland of collectivism, not to cringe before the bully of communism."

But these appeals were of no avail. Voters clearly wanted to honor the memory of the late President Kennedy (assassinated the previous November) and Goldwater's campaign had been disorganized from the start, failing to reach the hearts of the public. Even with the success of Reagan's "A Time for Choosing" speech – the "one bright spot in a dismal campaign," according to *Time* magazine,[2] bringing in several million dollars for the campaign in its last week – Barry Goldwater lost in a landslide. Johnson secured 61% of the popular vote, and all but six states and 52 electoral votes.

America's choice in 1964 was clear. Goldwater's conservative vision had been rejected by the American people.

● ● ●

Yet in defeat lay the seeds of future victory. Conservatives had failed to win the World Series of American politics, but

---

[2]   Peter Schweizer, *Reagan's War* (New York: Doubleday, 2002), p.44.

previously they had been a farm league team at best. In the pages of *National Review*, the leading magazine of the nascent conservative movement, Reagan himself wrote, shortly after the 1964 election, that a false image of conservativism had been routed, but not the philosophy itself.[3]

Just two years later, Reagan proved that conservatives could be elected, even in Democratic California, where he won the governorship over liberal incumbent Pat Brown by a margin equal to Johnson's 1964 presidential victory.

> There are no plans for retreating from our present positions, but we can't advance without reinforcements. Are reinforcements available? The answer is an unhesitating—"Yes!" They are to be found in the millions of so-called Republican defectors — those people who didn't really want LBJ, but who were scared of what they thought we represented. Read that sentence very carefully because in my opinion it tells the story. All of the landslide majority did not vote against the conservative philosophy, they voted against a false image our Liberal opponents successfully mounted.
>
> – Reagan writing about the meaning of Goldwater's loss in *National Review* (December 1, 1964)

Prominent California conservatives – such as Henry Salvatori, Holmes Tuttle, Ed Mills, and Cy Rubel, whom had originally put up the money to broadcast "A Time for Choosing" – had convinced Reagan to run for office in 1966. They recognized Reagan's substantial political talents: the trustworthiness he exhibited on the stump, his congenial nature that blunted charges of extremism, and his ability to put conservative principles into common-sense language that resonated with the public.

---

[3] "The Republican Party and the Conservative Movement," *National Review*, December 1, 1964, p. 55.

Adding fuel to the engine of the Reagan campaign were events of the day in California. From the start of his first term, Pat Brown had been an activist governor, using his early popularity to develop government initiatives intended to address a host of problems: consumer protection, fair employment, increased welfare, new public works construction, economic development, and expanding the state university system. But by the mid-60s, voters were upset by the impotence of Brown and the liberal establishment to solve the state's most pressing problem: escalating lawlessness. The problem was documented in statistics (FBI data showed crimes in California increased 72.5% between 1959 and 1964)[4] and visible in ugly student protests at Berkeley and then horrible race riots in the Watts section of Los Angeles that left 36 dead.

Brown, however, still approached the 1966 campaign with confidence. He didn't think Reagan was a serious candidate, and the state Republican Party was split between moderates and abrasive right-wing activists. It wouldn't be the last time Reagan was underestimated as a candidate, but he proved up to the challenge. To show he was capable and unscripted, he made himself available to reporters so they could see his mastery of the issues. To those who tried to portray Reagan as connected to John Birch Society extremists, he explained that if they wound up in his camp it meant they would "be buying my philosophy. I won't be buying theirs."[5] Reagan united a broad coalition of Californians – much as he did to win over "Reagan

---

[4]   Mathew Dallek, *The Right Moment* (New York: The Free Press, 2000), p. 198.
[5]   Lou Cannon, *Governor Reagan* (New York: PublicAffairs, 2003), p. 153.

Democrats" in his presidential runs – by focusing on broadly-held concerns while simultaneously offering an optimistic vision of how greatness could be restored.

Reagan won by nearly one million votes. A conservative political star was born.

California in 1966 provided a preview of the implosion of old Democratic coalitions that would soon occur on the national stage. While President Johnson got Congress to pass much of his agenda – including the creation of Medicare and expansions of the federal government's role in education, welfare, and other social programs – the Democratic Party was coming unglued, unable to hold together its traditional constituents while also appeasing the more radical "New Left." Richard Nixon exploited this political situation to win victories in the presidential elections of 1968 and 1972.

> There isn't anything we can't do, and that includes solving the one overriding issue of this campaign... the issue besetting not only California, but also the nation... the issue that overshadows and colors all others. It is the issue of simple morality. Who among us doesn't feel concern for the deterioration of old standards, the abandonment of principles time-tested and proven in our climb from the swamp to the stars? Today voices are raised urging change for change's sake. Individuals have privileges, but no responsibility. While some young Americans fight and die for their country, others send blood and money to the enemy, and what is, in truth, treason, is called their right to freedom of expression... Is this the way we want it to be? We can change it. We can start a prairie fire that will sweep the nation and prove we are number one in more than size and crime and taxes. If this is a dream, it's a good dream, as big and golden as California itself.
>
> – Reagan, campaigning on statewide television, September 9, 1966

But Nixon did not represent the conservative wing of the Republican Party, and his tenure in office would cede enormous ground to the liberal establishment. Nixon took a heavy-handed approach to economic issues, imposing counterproductive wage and price controls in 1971. He acquiesced to the creation of new regulatory agencies that would rope American businesses in red tape. His foreign policy centered on *detente* – the idea that we could create a workable balance of power with the Soviet empire – while also opening relations with China and its communist butcher of a leader, Mao Tse-Tung. And of course, Nixon's cynical attempt to cover up the Watergate scandal and to use the power of the federal government for personal political purposes exposed terrible disdain for the American Founders' vision of a limited government.

The Republican Party was decimated in the 1974 midterm elections that were held after Nixon resigned. Democrats picked up 42 seats in the House and four seats in the Senate to hold convincing majorities in both chambers.

Back in California, the election of 1974 marked the end of Reagan's two terms as governor. His successor was Democrat Jerry Brown, son of former Governor Pat Brown whom Reagan vanquished in 1966.

But Reagan's political career was hardly over. With the Republican Party in tatters, there was the possibility of taking it in a new direction, and Reagan was uniquely situated to lead the way. Beyond his personal charm and his experience as the chief executive of the largest state in the union, Reagan was becoming the leading national voice of conservativism.

From 1975 to 1979, except for the interlude of the 1976 campaign for the GOP presidential nomination, Reagan worked as a virtual one-man policy think tank. He expressed his views on the major foreign policy and domestic issues facing America in regular newspaper columns and daily radio commentary broadcasts. His commentaries would appear in 226 newspapers and be aired on 286 radio stations. During this period, friends and aids would later recall that Reagan was constantly writing on yellow legal pads his vision for America. [Of the more than 1,000 radio commentaries he would record during those four years, Reagan's own handwritten drafts of 670 have been found among his collection of private papers. Hundreds of these commentaries have been collected and reprinted in *Reagan, In His Own Hand*, dispelling the notion that Reagan was just an actor reading someone else's script.][6]

When Reagan wasn't communicating his message to regular Americans, he was speaking to conservative groups and trying to provide an ideological rudder for the wayward Republican Party. In 1975, Reagan discussed the heavy losses of the previous year's election, calling for greater commitment to conservative principles and for resisting the temptation to blur party distinctions:

> *A political party cannot be all things to all people. It must represent certain fundamental beliefs, which must not be compromised to political expediency, or simply to swell its numbers... And if there are those who cannot subscribe to these [conservative] principles, then let them go their way.*[7]

As the presidential election of 1976 neared, Reagan took the bold step of challenging incumbent President Gerald Ford

---

[6]   Kiron K. Skinner, Annelise Anderson, Martin Anderson (eds.), *Reagan: In His Own Hand* (New York: Simon & Schuster, 2001), pp. IX-XXiii and p. 503.

[7]   Reagan's speech at the March 1, 1975, meeting of the Conservative Political Action Committee, appears at: http://www.townhall.com/reagan/speeches/letthemgotheirway.htm

---

for the Republican nomination. Reagan looked certain to lose after setbacks in the early primaries, but, after vowing to compete to the very end, a series of Reagan upsets turned it into a remarkably close race. The nomination was decided at the convention, as Reagan tried to bring fence-sitting Ford delegates into his camp but wound up 70 votes short. In a closed-door speech to his supporters, he urged:

> *The cause goes on.... Nancy and I, we aren't going to go back and sit in a rocking chair on the front porch and say that's all for us... The cause will prevail because it is right. Don't give up your ideals. Don't compromise. Don't turn to expediency.*[8]

Indeed, in the years that followed, as Democrat Jimmy Carter assumed the presidency, Reagan would remain a vocal critic of the liberal policies and weak leadership that were driving the United States into deeper and deeper crises. The American military was in a state of neglect. The Soviet Union was on the advance, invading Afghanistan and fomenting communist revolution in Latin America and Africa. Radical Islamic fundamentalists, who had seized power in Iran in February 1979, took over the U.S. embassy in November of that year and held 52 Americans hostage. The one attempt at rescue pursued by Carter, in April 1980, failed and the dead bodies of American soldiers were dragged through the streets of Tehran.

At home, the economy was anemic. Inflation and unemployment both exceeded 10%, the prime interest rate reached 15%, and Americans faced another energy crisis.

---

[8] Peggy Noonan, *When Character Was King* (New York: Viking Press, 2001), pp.125-126.

Carter's ineptness in dealing with the nation's problems created another predicament, less tangible than the others, but perhaps even more important. In what came to be known as his "malaise speech" (though he never uses that term), Carter acknowledged "a crisis of confidence" threatening the United States. He spoke, "It is a crisis that strikes at the very heart and soul and spirit of our national will. We can see this crisis in the growing doubt about the meaning of our own lives and in the loss of a unity of purpose for our Nation. The erosion of our confidence in the future is threatening to destroy the social and the political fabric of America."[9]

> The first Republican president once said, "While the people retain their virtue and their vigilance, no administration by any extreme of wickedness or folly can seriously injure the government in the short space of four years."
>
> If Mr. Lincoln could see what's happened in these last three-and-a-half years, he might hedge a little on that statement.
>
> – Reagan, speech to the Republican National Convention, July 17, 1980.

In November 1979, Reagan announced his candidacy for the presidency, seeking to settle unfinished business from 1976. The central theme of his campaign would be renewing America's confidence in itself. And over the course of the following twelve months, Reagan earned the confidence of the American people in his leadership and laid the groundwork for the most significant political change in the United States in 50 years.

Reagan turned the election into a referendum on Carter's term in office, asking voters, "Are you better off now

---

[9] Carter's speech of July 15, 1979, appears at: http://www.usembassy.de/usa/etexts/speeches/rhetoric/jccrisis.htm.

than you were four years ago?" Since Carter had few victories to celebrate and fewer new ideas for the future, his only strategy was to paint Reagan as reckless and irresponsible. Carter's pollster Patrick Caddell explained the "attack Reagan" strategy years later, "We didn't have any card to play because there wasn't any cards (sic) to play."[10]

When Reagan had the chance to debate Carter face to face, a week before election day, he rebuffed Carter's distortions of his record (famously correcting Carter with a dismissive line, "There you go again," late in the debate). Reagan promised "to take Government off the backs of the great people of this country, and turn you loose again to do those things that I know you can do so well, because you did them and made this country great."[11]

Reagan won the 1980 election by more than 8 million votes. The electoral vote margin, 489-49, recalled the historic 472-59 mandate Franklin D. Roosevelt received when turning Herbert Hoover out of office in 1932. The Reagan Revolution had begun.

● ● ●

On January 20, 1981, as Reagan stepped forward to put his hand on his mother's Bible and take the oath of office, the sun was beginning to peek through the day's overcast skies. So too, it seemed, for the entire nation. The Iranian hostage crisis ended that day; and, on the steps of the Capitol, Reagan used his inaugural address to pledge to reverse the

---

10 Glenn Garvin, "New insight into Carter White House," *The Miami Herald,* November 11, 2002.
11 A transcript of the 1980 debate between Carter and Reagan appears at: http://www.debates.org/pages/trans80b.html

decades-old course of dramatically growing the federal government:

> *We as Americans have the capacity now, as we've had in the past, to do whatever needs to be done to preserve this last and greatest bastion of freedom. In this present crisis, government is not the solution to our problem; government is the problem. From time to time we've been tempted to believe that society has become too complex to be managed by self-rule, that government by an elite group is superior to government for, by, and of the people. Well, if no one among us is capable of governing himself, then who among us has the capacity to govern someone else?*

At the outset of his remarks, Reagan marveled at how commonplace seems the peaceful transfer of power under the U.S. Constitution, but how unique and special it is in the history of man. In a similar vein, no one was surprised by what Reagan said that day – "vintage Reagan" remarked *The Washington Post*[12] – but his speech was a historical watershed.

> *We are a nation that has a government – not the other way around. And this makes us special among the nations of the Earth. Our government has no power except that granted it by the people. It is time to check and reverse the growth of government, which shows signs of having grown beyond the consent of the governed.*

With Reagan's call to reduce the size and power of the federal government came an appreciation for the quiet heroism of everyday Americans and a departure from the Carter Administration's rhetoric about lowered expectations.

---

[12] "Inaugural Address: Evocative Version of Campaign Message," *The Washington Post*, January 21, 1981.

If we look to the answer as to why for so many years we achieved so much, prospered as no other people on Earth, it was because here in this land we unleashed the energy and individual genius of man to a greater extent than has ever been done before. Freedom and the dignity of the individual have been more available and assured here than in any other place on Earth. The price for this freedom at times has been high, but we have never been unwilling to pay that price.

It is no coincidence that our present troubles parallel and are proportionate to the intervention and intrusion in our lives that result from unnecessary and excessive growth of government. It is time for us to realize that we're too great a nation to limit ourselves to small dreams. We're not, as some would have us believe, doomed to an inevitable decline. I do not believe in a fate that will fall on us no matter what we do. I do believe in a fate that will fall on us if we do nothing. So, with all the creative energy at our command, let us begin an era of national renewal. Let us renew our determination, our courage, and our strength. And let us renew our faith and our hope.

Reagan's vision was clear from day one, but he faced an uphill battle to enact it. The House of Representatives remained in Democrats' hands. Curing inflation would require swallowing bitter economic medicine that would trigger a temporary recession. The liberal media was, by nature, suspicious of the changes Reagan intended to bring to foreign policy.

Reagan was almost robbed of the chance to press for his agenda. Just two months into his presidency, on March 30, 1981, Reagan was nearly assassinated outside the Washington Hilton, where John Hinckley put a bullet an inch from his heart. This near tragedy would actually turn into a major political victory for Reagan as the American people began to learn of the anecdotes of his toughness and humor during this moment of life-threatening trauma. (To the doctors about to operate on him, he joked: "I just hope you're all Republicans." Later, to the staff members who assured him the government was running as usual: "What makes you think that would make me feel better?")

For Reagan personally, the assassination attempt would be a life altering event. It imbued him with an even greater sense of urgency, determination, and purpose. Always a religious man, Reagan believed he had been spared by God for a purpose – a thought seconded by Mother Teresa months later when she visited the White House. "This has happened to you at this time because your country and the world need you," she said.[13]

Four and a half months after the Hinckley shooting, Reagan would sign into law the largest tax cut in American history, which reduced personal income taxes across the board by an average of 25 percent.[14] He would also fire air traffic controllers waging an illegal strike. This was politically unpopular in the short term, but very valuable for Reagan in the long-term, sending a message (to foreign adversaries as well as political rivals) not to call his bluff – Reagan's words would be met by action.

Budget deficits started to increase – a result of Reagan's big increases in defense spending, his budget compromises with the Democratic House (Reagan slowed the rate of non-defense spending, but could not pare it back), and an economy

---

[13] Dinesh D'Souza, *Ronald Reagan: How an Ordinary Man Became an Extraordinary Leader* (New York: The Free Press, 1997), p. 207.
[14] "The Tax Cut and You: How it Works," The Associated Press, August 13, 1981.

in recession. Reagan's approval ratings by January 1983 fell to 35%, but he remained confident in his conservative vision and the difficult decisions he had made. In a press conference at the midpoint of his first term, he remarked:

> *My greatest satisfaction is the conviction that a country that was skidding dangerously in the wrong direction, losing the respect of friends and foes alike in the world and, even worse, losing faith in its own future, has been set on the right course. We've begun to undo the damage that the overtaxing, overspending, over-regulating binge of the sixties and seventies inflicted on the American way of life, and we've made America respected in the world again. My biggest regret is that because the accumulated damages piled up so high for so long, putting America's house in order has been a tough and painful task.* [15]

Reagan soon would be vindicated, as the economic pain of 1982 gave way to the country's longest peacetime economic expansion.

Reagan would continue to face difficult tests throughout his presidency, especially in charting a new course in the Cold War and reasserting American leadership on the world stage. In 1983 alone, Reagan dealt with the Soviet Union downing a commercial Korean airliner with 61 Americans and 208 others aboard, the killing of 282 American servicemen in a terrorist attack in Lebanon, and a communist threat in the small Caribbean nation of Grenada. In the same year, he took an unpopular stand in deploying Pershing II missiles in Western Europe; was chastised for calling the Soviet Union "an evil empire"; and introduced a Strategic Defense Initiative (SDI) to build a system to shoot down missiles in a

---

[15] Reagan's press conference of January 20, 1983, is transcribed at: http://www.reagan.utexas.edu/resource/speeches/1983/12083a.htm.

nuclear attack, which was ridiculed in the media as his "Star Wars" program. A poll in February 1984 indicated the American public disapproved of Reagan's foreign policy by a 5:4 margin.

By Election Day 1984, however, it would be a different story. Americans would again ask themselves if they were better off than they were four years ago and, this time, the answer was a resounding yes. Reagan won re-election in a landslide; the electoral count was 525 to 13. Four years under Reagan had again made the country prosperous, strong and proud.

During Reagan's second term, the economy continued to boom and American patriotism surged. At the nation celebrated the 100th anniversary of the Statue of Liberty in 1986, Reagan's approval ratings climbed to 68%.

Months later, however, Reagan's popularity was wounded by the Iran-Contra scandal, involving arms sales to enemies in Iran, in a misguided effort to win release of American hostages and then transfer proceeds to anti-communist insurgents in Nicaragua. Reagan cooperated with investigators and was cleared of wrongdoing, but the incident reflected poor judgment in his administration.

Also hurting Reagan's approval ratings in this period was the perceived failure of a major summit with Soviet Premier Mikhail Gorbachev in Iceland. Reagan walked way from an offer to dramatically slash inventories of nuclear arms, because it was conditional on abandoning SDI.

Reagan had calculated from the beginning of his administration that the Soviet Union's economy was more dysfunctional than commonly believed. He suspected it could not support an arms race with the United States, especially if tasked with the research and development of a transformative military technology like SDI. Something would have to give.

In the end, Gorbachev returned to the negotiating table, desperate for an excuse to decrease military spending, making the same concessions without asking Reagan to give up SDI. Gorbachev would receive most of the credit for the relaxation of tensions between the United States and the Soviet Union – in 1989, *Time* would name him "Man of the Decade" – but it was Ronald Reagan who dictated the terms of the most sweeping military disarmament in history.

> There's no limit to what a man can do or where he can go if he doesn't mind who gets the credit.
>
> – words engraved on a small plaque that Reagan kept on his Oval Office desk.

So let's review. How did Reagan do?

"Not bad. Not bad at all," he reflected in his farewell address in 1989.

Reagan entered office in 1981 with inflation out of control at 12%. His economic policy arrested the problem and by the end of 1982 inflation was just 4%, a level that would be sustained throughout his presidency.

When he entered office, the top marginal tax rate was 78%, which meant that a worker in that bracket would receive less than a quarter of every additional dollar earned. Reagan slashed all tax rates, cutting the top rate by more than half to 35%. The stock market tripled from the time Reagan entered office to the time he left it. Hundreds of new companies were born, creating millions of jobs and entire new industries that signaled the beginning of the information technology boom.

Unemployment peaked above 10% in 1982, and then fell to 5.4%. Interest rates were cut in half. Oil prices plummeted after Reagan deregulated them. Growth in non-military federal spending was reigned in (though not as much as desired) and federal regulation was reduced by about 40,000 pages in the Federal Register.

Just as important as reviving the country's economic might, Reagan also revived the spirit of the American people. The rest of the world took note. In praising America's institutions of freedom, Reagan drew a stark contrast with the world's tyrannies and terrorists. Reagan's moral clarity in foreign affairs drew scorn among so-called sophisticates at *The New York Times* – "Primitive, that is the only word for it," columnist Anthony Lewis editorialized about Reagan's "evil empire" speech[16] – but, by denying the legitimacy of unelected dictators, Reagan gave hope to dissidents yearning for freedom throughout the communist empire.

Reagan succeeded in turning the tide of the Cold War. Unlike his predecessors, Reagan believed it was possible to defeat, not just contain, communism. When Reagan exited office in 1989, the dispirited leadership of the Soviet Union was relaxing its grip on its East European satellites and retreating from its war of conquest in Afghanistan. The Berlin Wall would fall later that year, and on Christmas Day 1991, the Soviet Union itself would dissolve.

● ● ●

---

[16] Anthony Lewis, "Onward Christian Soldiers," *New York Times*, November 21, 1983.

In the years since 1989, key Reaganite principles – peace through strength, free market economics – have become the conventional wisdom to such an extent that it is easy to forget how dramatic Reagan's policy changes were.

Unfortunately, political leaders of our current era largely have failed to push the Reagan Revolution further.

> In closing, let me thank you, the American people, for giving me the great honor of allowing me to serve as your president. When the Lord calls me home, whenever that day may be, I will leave with the greatest love for this country of ours and eternal optimism for its future.
>
> I now begin the journey that will lead me into the sunset of my life. I know that for America there will always be a bright dawn ahead.
>
> – closing paragraphs of Reagan's letter to the American people, November 5, 1994

The first President Bush was never an ideological heir to Reagan, confessing that he lacked "the vision thing." After breaking his pledge not to raise taxes, the economy slumped in 1991. These economic woes, and the sudden evaporation of the United States's Cold War foe, opened the door for Bill Clinton's victory in 1992. Clinton won running as a "New Democrat," adopting conservative language in his pledges to reform welfare, stay tough on crime, and bring fiscal responsibility. Whether he could have won the election without third-party candidate Ross Perot claiming 19% of the popular vote (mostly from Republican ranks) remains an open question. Clinton was reminded of the mood of the electorate in 1994 when the public reacted negatively to his administration's big government health care plan, sweeping Republicans into control of the House and Senate for the first time in 40 years.

Just days before this Republican victory, President Reagan addressed the American people for the last time, in the form of a courageous open letter announcing he had been diagnosed with Alzheimer's disease. Reagan explained that it was his hope by openly sharing his condition with the public would draw attention to the crippling disease that robs millions of Americans of their memories and their faculties during their last years of life. Reagan's final words to the American people radiated the same characteristics Americans had come to know over Reagan's decades in the public eye: courage, dignity, and a profound sense of optimism.

Reagan exited the public stage to a life of quiet privacy, under the care of his loving wife, Nancy.

• • •

The 1990s were, in the words of George Will, a "holiday from history"[17] as politicians stopped dealing with hard questions because they didn't have to. Expanding global trade and Internet-era productivity gains brought unprecedented wealth. Except for a few regional conflicts, the world appeared quiet.

Rhetorically at least, the "era of big government [was] over," even according to President Clinton, but the public had little appetite to make fundamental changes in government. Instead, they watched politicians jockey for power in a nation evenly split among Republicans and Democrats. More often than not, the arguments were fueled by the relentless sequence of scandals coming from the Clinton White House.

It was never clear at the time what Clinton meant with his 1996 campaign tagline about "building a bridge to the

---

[17] George Will, "The End of Our Holiday from History," *The Washington Post*, September 12, 2001.

21st Century." But from this side of that millennial divide, we can see that Clinton's bridge was built from the cans he kicked down the road for the next president to address: a gathering terrorist threat, a nuclear arms program in North Korea, tyrants in rogue states pursuing weapons of mass destruction, renewed violence in Israel, unreformed entitlement programs at home, litigation gone mad, an ethical vacuum in which corporate scandals flourished, a stock market bubble about to burst, and a lingering crisis in inner-city public education.

These are the problems that George W. Bush inherited after the incredibly tight election of 2000. The terrorist attacks of September 11, 2001, of course, have very much defined Bush's first term in office. The vision, moral clarity, and determination he has exhibited in waging a war on global terror to prevent further attacks has won him admiration among conservatives and, more generally, the American people who gave Republicans major victories in 2002's midterm elections.

On other fronts, however, Bush has conceded ground to the liberal establishment. Discretionary non-military spending jumped 30% from 2000 to 2003. Bush signed into law a campaign finance reform bill he believed to be unconstitutional. In the areas of education and health care, Bush has fought for big and costly government programs. Bush's 2002 tax cuts were certainly Reaganesque, but as we go to print in 2004, he still has not used his presidential veto power to stand up for conservative ideas.

The recent death of Ronald Reagan provides needed perspective on our current situation. A great deal of progress has been made since Reagan stepped on the political stage during the Goldwater campaign 40 years ago, but we may be in danger of complacency. What good is it to have Republicans controlling government if that power does not yield real results?

We face another "Time for Choosing." Will our era go down in history as the time that Republicans became content to preside over the status quo? Or will we continue to fight for Reagan's vision of America as a city on a hill, a model of freedom that will inspire the rest of the world? The answer to this question depends on our actions in the months and years to come.

Chapter 2

The Battle for Freedom at Home

The Reagan Revolution should teach conservatives one key lesson: Success is achieved by sticking to our principles.

Forget trying to please the media establishment. Forget the cynical political strategies of "triangulation." When Americans are presented with common-sense conservative ideas, they tend to vote for them. In those cases where conservative ideas are ahead of popular opinion – as still may be the case with school choice, for example – we cannot shy away from tough political battles. We might lose in the short term, but we know our ideas will be vindicated by time and experience. Moreover, respect will be won by standing on principle.

Of course, this is easier said than done. Sometimes issues in Washington become so muddled, it is difficult even to discern how best to stand for conservative principles. Harder still, it requires a great deal of courage to keep standing for those principles when the media elite and the special interest groups want nothing more than for you to go back to sitting silently in the corner.

Dinesh D'Souza, author of the excellent Reagan biography *How an Ordinary Man Became an Extraordinary Leader*, suggests that the best way to gather the wisdom and courage to effectively fight for conservative positions is "to ask in every situation that arises, *what would Reagan have done?*"[18]

In this chapter, we look at today's domestic policy issues to identify Reaganite solutions that ought to be advanced by conservatives in this election season and in the years to come. Reagan's long career of speeches, writings, and actions in office provides us with ample opportunities to learn Reagan's perspective on nearly all the important issues of the day.

We can also draw conclusions based on Reagan's general approach to politics. During the 1984 campaign, Reagan defined his philosophy on governance: "Four years ago we began to navigate by certain fixed principles. Freedom was our North Star, and common sense our constellations."[19] When we develop policy recommendations and strategies, we ought to remember this *North Star Rule*: Our goal is to maximize individual freedom, while understanding that common sense will require certain compromises to protect our security and fulfill existing obligations the government has assumed.

The act of "navigating" toward a goal concedes that our journey may be a lengthy one. While en route, policy options

---

[18] Dinesh D'Souza, *Ronald Reagan: How an Ordinary Man Became an Extraordinary Leader* (The Free Press: 1997), p. 264.

[19] Reagan's speech in Saginaw, Michigan, of November 2, 1984, is published among The Public Papers of President Ronald W. Reagan, at: http://www.reagan.utexas.edu/resource/speeches/1984/110284a.htm.

that are less-than-perfect may offer real progress in the right direction. The important thing is to never cede ground to opponents who want to grow government at the expense of individual liberty.

Reagan had a brilliant knack for creating a consensus in the direction of greater freedom. Not only would he find the "sweet spot" of an issue, where reasonable policy solutions could be devised to move debate in a conservative direction. Reagan also knew how to communicate to the American people in a way that appealed to their intuitive sense of what's fair, what works, and what's best for their country.

So let's go a step beyond "*what would Reagan have done?*" and ask also, "*what would Reagan have said?*" After all, understanding the conservative perspective on domestic policy issues will not re-ignite the Reagan Revolution. Understanding the philosophy is the easy part. The challenge comes in articulating policy goals in a manner that can win the hearts and minds of most Americans. After all, Barry Goldwater, Ronald Reagan and Newt Gingrich had very similar visions for the country. But Reagan was much more successful in marketing that vision and connecting with the American people.

What was his secret? First, Reagan sincerely respected his fellow Americans. He was fond of recalling Thomas Jefferson belief that "If the people know all the facts, the people will never make a mistake."[20]

---

[20] Reagan, "Remarks at an Exhibit of Weapons Captured in Central America" of March 13, 1986. Published among The Presidential Papers of Ronald W. Reagan at: http://www.reagan.utexas.edu/resource/speeches/1986/31386c.htm

Because of this, Reagan would look for where the true problem lies and find the facts that make this case, and the real-life anecdotes that drove home the relevance of the problem to the citizens in his audience.

There are just too many people in this town who think this money belongs to the government. Well, it doesn't. It's your money. It's your sons' and daughters' money that they're hoping to use for a new home. It's your parents' money that they need for a decent retirement. And if we do nothing else in this administration, we're going to convince this city that the power, the money, and the responsibility in this country begins and ends with the people and not with some cinderblock building in Washington, D.C.

– From the speech Reagan gave just before being shot by John Hinckley on May 30, 1981. Reagan's audience was a division of the AFL-CIO, not a friendly audience to Republicans. Reagan used an anecdote about a laid-off Peoria construction worker and this type of moral argument to appeal to the hearts and minds of his audience.

With the facts on his side, Reagan might have been tempted to merely make the pragmatic case for his proposed policy solution, but he almost always went beyond this and made a moral argument. He knew Americans have a great appreciation for individual freedom, dignity and responsibility. Thus, President Reagan was careful to not simply describe tax reductions as good for the economy. He declared that it was simply wrong for the government to take an unreasonable percentage of what anyone earned.

This is important distinction. Two years passed before the economy took off as a result of Reagan's tax reforms, but that time lag—even if it had taken a decade—would not have changed the moral case for lower taxes.

Finally, Reagan always radiated optimism, trustworthiness, and confidence. These traits – common to most great leaders – came naturally to Reagan, and they helped him win votes even among people who did not consider themselves conservatives at all. Reagan never embraced the title he was given as the "Great Communicator," insisting instead that he merely "communicated great things," but we should not underestimate how much his policy successes were due to his quick wit, humility, and ability to clearly articulate his vision for America.

Few of us will ever match Reagan's talents at public speaking or putting our thoughts on paper, but we can think methodically about how to package a message to inspire our fellow citizens – whether they are members of a congressional committee or neighbors next door.

As we examine the policy challenges that face us, we have to ask ourselves:

- Have we presented the facts that best make the case for a policy reform?

- Have we explained the moral case to remind our audience that freedom is our North Star?

- Finally, are we appealing to the natural optimism and decency of the American people and demonstrating our sincere desire in the public interest?

Our challenge is to re-ignite the ideas of the Reagan Revolution. We can do it if we pay careful attention to the words and actions of Reagan himself.

Getting Government Off People's Backs

Everyone who wishes to build a better society in the dawning 21st Century should bear in mind the central lesson of the century that just ended. That is: Capitalist, free-market economies create prosperity, raise living standards, and allow for greater exercise of individual rights. By contrast, the 20th Century's big-government experiments in collectivism – whether it's the national socialism of Nazi Germany and fascist Italy; the communist totalitarianism of the Soviet Union, Mao's China, Castro's Cuba, and Pol Pot's Cambodia; or even softer forms of welfare state socialism, like Great Britain before Margaret Thatcher – were resounding failures.

This lesson had no better teacher than Ronald Reagan.

Reagan understood that, when government promises to achieve economic security and equality, it only produces an equality of poverty and dependency. In 1964, the consensus wisdom ran opposite to what we know now, but Reagan was resolute in describing the country's choice as one between the individualism inherent in the American Dream and a collectivism that submits to an aloof government elite.

> Today, the world is divided between those who believe in the free marketplace and those who believe in government control and ownership of the economy.
>
> – from Reagan's radio commentary, "Free Enterprise," April 16, 1979
>
> (*In His Own Hand*, p. 228)

Reagan believed people are able to look after their own affairs without government interference, except in rare circumstances. Too many leaders of Reagan's day and our own assume government should play a paternal role, telling "the masses" what to do, and looking out for the "common man." Reagan scoffed at terms like this because he believed individual Americans were very uncommon. [21] Most individuals lead lives of quiet dignity: raising families, working hard and saving what they can, giving time and effort to their local communities.

Originally a New Deal Democrat, Reagan believed government has a role to play in creating a safety net for the truly needy. But when government increases its involvement too much, it can make life *more* difficult for individual Americans. Politicians had sold the expansion of government as new benefits that would achieve a Great Society, but the reality has been higher taxes, new limitations on individual choices, and greater dependency on the decisions of distant bureaucrats who can never be as effective and responsive to needs as local charities.

Today, consider how much of your life is spent jumping through government hoops.

At age six, you are assigned a seat in a school paid for and run by the government. Unless your family can afford paying for private school on top of the taxes they paid for public school, you will probably be in that school system for the next 12 years. Whether or not you learn the skills necessary to succeed later in life is in large part dependent on the workings of a system run by the same folks, as Reagan might say, "who brought us the postal service and Amtrak."[22]

During your working years, the average American family faces a total tax burden of over 38%. That means every time you earn three dollars, the government is taking back more than one from you. On average, American families

---

[21] Ronald Reagan, "Looking Out a Window," radio commentary of January 27, 1978, collected in *Reagan In His Own Hand*, p. 18.

[22] Ronald Reagan, "Socialized Medicine," radio commentary of July 6, 1977, collected in *Reagan In His Own Hand*, p. 366.

give the government more of their earnings than they spend on food, clothing and housing combined.[23]

We have a government that spends $2.3 trillion dollars in a single year. That's another $4.3 million every minute that goes by. How did this happen? Figuring this out is essential to our task of ultimately reversing the trend.

Let's look at one example: the 2002 Farm Bill, which passed with strong support from both Republicans and Democrats. The price tag on this one is $171 billion over the next ten years. Divide that by the number of taxpaying households, and your family's share is about $4,400.[24]

The Farm Bill provides subsidies to farmers, presumably to keep unprofitable ones from slipping into bankruptcy. Different amounts are doled out depending on the types and amount of crops produced. Despite legislators' tear-jerking stories about helping to keep poor family farmers out of poverty, the bulk of subsidies go to large, wealthy farmers and businesses. Ninety percent of all farm subsidies go to growers of corn, wheat, cotton, soybeans, and rice. Large producers, which are typically the most profitable, receive the greatest subsidies. Nearly three-quarters of the most recent farm subsidies went to just ten percent of recipients.

This is important because it's an example of a government program with "diffused costs" and "concentrated benefits." You and I share the burden of increased government spending for the Farm Bill, about $440 per year

---

[23] "Tax Facts," Americans for Tax Reform. See: http://www.atr.org/talkingpoints/110101taxfacts.html.

[24] "Still at the Federal Trough: Farm Subsidies for the Rich and Famous Shattered Records in 2001," *Backgrounder*, The Heritage Foundation, April 30, 2002, p. 1.

for each taxpayer. That's enough to make us angry now, but it wasn't enough to make us drop what we were doing and lobby against the Farm Bill when it was being considered. By contrast, ten percent of recipients from the farm bill will receive more than $250,000 each year. Needless to say, those people were very active in lobbying for the bill, and will work diligently to ensure that this policy continues.

The problem of diffused costs and concentrated benefits is at the root of the problem of big government spending. Each program has a very motivated recipient that stands to gain big, and millions of taxpayers who, because they only lose a little per person, have few advocates speaking out on their behalf. This is how the federal government winds up paying for things like $500,000 for catfish health in Stoneville, Mississippi; one million dollars for a DNA study of bears in Montana; and, four million dollars for the International Fertilizer Development Center.[25]

We hear much of special interest groups. Well, our concern must be for a special interest group that has been too long neglected. It knows no sectional boundaries or ethnic and racial divisions, and it crosses political party lines. It is made up of men and women who raise our food, patrol our streets, man our mines and factories, teach our children, keep our homes, and heal us when we're sick — professionals, industrialists, shopkeepers, clerks, cabbies, and truck-drivers. They are, in short, "We the people," this breed called Americans.

— from Reagan's First Inaugural, January 20, 1981

---

[25] "CAGW Identifies Record $22.5 Billion in Pork," press release from Citizens Against Government Waste, April 9, 2003. Available online: http://www.cagw.org/site Page Server? pagename=news NewsRelease 04092003

Conservatives who wish to reignite the Reagan Revolution have to stop aiding and abetting this kind of pork barrel spending. Let's have a renewed focus on how waste can be cut from the government budget.

The facts are certainly on our side. Conservatives making this case to the public should contrast the silliness of these spending ideas with the very grave challenges that government should be addressing.

As we wage the War on Terror, eliminating pork is a patriotic duty. What legislator can sleep with good conscience if funds are being wasted on political patronage when we could be shoring up critical areas of responsibility in intelligence, defense, and homeland security? It's become fashionable for congressional representatives to wear American flags on their lapels. Americans should demand patriotism not only in fashion but in action. "Just say no to pork" should become a national rallying cry.

Conservatives can make these arguments confident that they are serving the public interest. Government spending often creates results completely at odds with what is desired. Beyond the obscene price tag, the Farm Bill distorts incentives and thereby leads to the over-production of some crops. Other countries' farmers (who don't get Farm Bill subsidies) find they can't compete against the subsidized American farmers and go out of business. As a consequence, many countries of the world have closed agricultural sectors and stay reliant on foreign aid (again, usually paid for out of the pockets of American taxpayers). They refuse to lower their barriers to America's most competitive exports until our agriculture subsidies are eliminated.

In a free market, without Farm Bill subsidies, farmers would be focused on meeting the needs of consumers, not government bureaucrats. American exporters would gain access to new foreign markets, increase their sales, and hire new workers. A few currently-subsidized domestic producers would miss the current gravy train, but those who serve customers best would prosper.

The general economy stands to benefit when we stop giving incentives for unproductive activities. In other words, Republicans should reform corporate welfare just as they tackled individual welfare. When President Clinton signed the 1996 Welfare Reform Act into law, most Democrats were convinced misery was just around the corner. But as incentives shifted away from idleness and towards work, most welfare recipients were able to find productive employment and were put on a path to self-sufficiency and greater personal fulfillment.[26] The same can happen for businesses that have become dependent on government.

Now, there is a limit to the impact we can achieve by eliminating pork barrel spending from the budget. The large majority of the budget – more than 60% – is considered "non-discretionary" because it supports entitlement programs and pays interest on the national debt. Of the 39.4% of the budget

---

[26] Welfare reform provides a good example for how policymakers can successfully implement reform that are both guided by a North Star and created based on common sense. Welfare reform's North Star was the principle that able-bodied individual ought not be wards of the state since it was unfair to those working to support themselves and to those who receive assistance since it inevitably saps their self respect. But common sense required that programs be put in place to assist those currently receiving assistance and to those who temporarily fall on hard times. The welfare bill included investments in job training and provisions for daycare facilities to help former welfare recipients embark on a path toward self-sufficiency. The success of this reform process should inspire policymakers to craft proposals that embrace both principles. More information is available from The Heritage Foundation at: http://www.heritage.org/Research/Welfare/bg1620.cfm.

that Congress can easily affect, more than half of that amount is spent on defense.[27]

However, spending on wasteful programs does add up. Eliminating the $22.5 billion in 2003 which the nonprofit group, Citizens Against Government Waste, identified as pork barrel spending would have a significant impact on the deficit. Perhaps more important than the actual money being saved, eliminating this spending would prevent the federal government's increased meddling in local areas that are outside its proper sphere of authority.

Freeing the Productive Spirits of Americans

A common-sense rollback of corporate welfare and pork barrel spending would be a great start for achieving a new conservative agenda. To really accelerate our country's economic potential, however, we must address other areas of public policy that constrain the productive spirit of Americans.

While corporations certainly don't deserve a hand-out, neither do they deserve the heavy-handed treatment they get from government regulators. The total cost of complying with the sum of federal regulations was estimated at $843 billion in 2000. For businesses, these costs translate into nearly $5,000 per employee. Small businesses are

---

[27] Using 2002 statistics from the U.S. Office of Management and Budget, *Historical Tables: Budget of the United States Government 2004*, appearing online at: http://www.whitehouse.gov/omb/budget/fy2004/pdf/hist.pdf.

disproportionately affected, with costs of nearly $7,000 per employee.[28]

Some regulations are prudent, but many are just plain unnecessary. There are more than 75,000 pages in the Federal Register, which lists all of the rules which have the force of law. The Cato Institute's publication, *Ten Thousand Commandments: An Annual Snapshot of the Federal Regulatory State*, identifies numerous pending government proposals to regulate the absolute minutiae of our daily lives and economy.[29]

Even in areas of life where most Americans are thankful to have a "watchdog" looking out for safety, we have to question whether the government is serving the public interest in its regulator role. For instance, before a company can sell a new pharmaceutical in the United States, it must get approval from the Food and Drug Administration. The FDA understandably errs on the side of caution, as none of its employees wants to be held responsible in public for approving a drug that later is determined to have harmful side effects. But there is a downside in this bias against approving new drugs. We never hear about all the people who suffer, or die, waiting for pharmaceuticals to come to market – people who might choose to risk negative side-effects in order to try a potentially life-saving solution. As Robert Goldberg of Brandeis University notes: "By a conservative

---

[28] W. Mark Crain and Thomas D. Hopkins, "The Impact of Regulatory Costs on Small Firms," The Office of Advocacy, U.S. Small Business Administration, RFP No. SBAHQ-00-R-0027, 2001, p. 7-9. Available at: http://www.sba.gov/advo/research/rs207tot.pdf.

[29] Clyde Wayne Crews, "Washington's Ten Thousand Commandments — and What to Do About Them," Cato Institute, July 10, 2003. Available online: http://www.cato.org/dailys/07-10-03-2.html.

estimate, FDA delays in allowing U.S. marketing of drugs used safely and effectively elsewhere around the world have cost the lives of at least 200,000 Americans over the past 30 years."[30]

The culture of risk-averse regulation needs to be changed. The burden of proof ought to be on regulators to show the benefits of regulation outweigh the costs, both direct and indirect. Perhaps there would be less public indifference to this problem of business regulation if more conservatives were vocal in defending the free enterprise system in general.

Republicans are often tagged by adversaries as "the party of business." Conservatives should wear that label as a badge of honor, and explain why. Businesses reflect the genius of ordinary people to create things that others value. The only businesses that succeed are ones that people willingly pay in exchange for goods and services they desire. Government, of course, doesn't care whether you are satisfied or not with their services. It just threatens jail time if you don't hand over your money every April 15.

Those who vilify big business are making a big mistake. Granted, some businesses seek favors from government – subsidies (i.e., corporate welfare) as we've discussed, or even regulations written in ways that hurt their competitors more than themselves – and for these we should have no sympathy. But some politicians, such as Al Gore in his 2000 Presidential campaign, seem to think you can stick it to big business without sticking it to the American people.

---

[30] Doug Bandow, "The FDA can be Dangerous to Your Health," Cato Institute, January 29, 1997, available online at: http://www.cato.org/dailys/1-29-97.html.

Ronald Reagan used one of his radio commentaries to explain an elementary concept of economics, by exploring the example of a corner grocery store.[31] The patrons of the store understand that the grocer must charge enough to cover the wholesale price of the goods, wages of workers, his mortgage for the building, and a fair return for himself to make a living. In other words, all the costs that go into running a business must be paid for by its customers or else the business will fail.

When you're adding up those costs, don't forget about government. If the government were to impose a property tax on the building, the burden of that tax would naturally be passed on to the consumer. Same goes for other taxes paid (and passed on) by the grocery store's own vendors: the sales tax the farmer paid on seeds is priced into the crops he sells, and the trucker builds gasoline taxes into his pricing for bringing products to the market. "What all this adds up to," Reagan explained, "is that government can't tax things like businesses or corporations, it can only tax people."

Voters would be very reluctant to punish big business if they understood that it really meant punishing consumers like themselves. When government increases the costs of buying and selling goods, through taxes or regulation, it effectively decreases the wealth available for individuals to spend, save, and invest.

This takes us right into the debate over taxation. Reagan understood that America's economic greatness is driven by individuals – individuals who take risks as entrepreneurs and investors, who work overtime to meet a deadline or get

---

[31] Ronald Reagan, "Economics I," radio commentary of July 31, 1978, collected in *Reagan In His Own Hand*, p. 258.

ahead, who make markets work by shopping for the most competitive products.

When government takes too much money out of the hands of individuals, there are fewer resources available to start new businesses or patronize existing ones. When incentives discourage earning more, the American economy is bound to fall short of its potential. When the tax code is a muddle of complicated credits and penalties, taxpayers will spend money and effort looking for loopholes and doing things just for the sake of lowering their tax bill.

When Reagan was President, he made taxes lower, simpler, and fairer. His 1981 Economic Recovery Act was the largest tax cut in U.S. history. It triggered an economic revival from the doldrums of the Carter era, launching a period of prosperity that many have called the "Long Boom."

Reagan's principles for tax reform are the same prescription for reform we need today. Taxes should be made more transparent. Taxes should be lower and flatter, so as not to discourage work. Savings and investment should not be discouraged through the tax code.

Well-meaning fiscal conservatives often focus on the need to balance the budget and argue that we ought to forego tax cuts until we achieve that goal. Reagan's experience serves as an example. While tax cuts may cause government's revenues to drop initially, they trigger growth in the overall economy so, in future years, more revenue is collected using lower rates.

Over the ten years that followed the Reagan's tax cuts, government revenue *grew* by more than $1 trillion.[32] During

---

[32] "Government Revenues Increased Over $1 Trillion in Years Following 1981-83 Tax Cut," Heritage Foundation (see http://www.heritage.org/Research/Taxes/images/chart.gif)

Reagan's tenure in office, government tax receipts to the federal government actually doubled. The cause of the deficit was Reagan's military buildup and the increases in domestic spending that Congress demanded in exchange for approving Reagan's desired defense spending.

Deficits are never desirable, but Reagan accepted them as a cost of changing the course of the Cold War, and predicted that the United States. would grow through them. That's exactly what happened. With restraint imposed on government spending (albeit temporarily) after Republicans won Congress in 1994, and the tech boom beginning to accelerate, the growth in the economy simply outpaced the growth in government, yielding surpluses in the late 1990s.

When you are steering a ship, you keep your eyes on your destination at the horizon line, rather than focus on every approaching wave. The lesson of Reagan's economic policy is the same: Aligning incentives for long-term economic growth is more important than obsessing over the temporary fluctuations that inevitably occur.

Putting Power Back in the Hands of the People

Reagan's belief in the power of individuals, and dangers of government interventions, has implications beyond economics. Let's look at one aspect to American society where there is a high degree of consensus over the goal, but much disagreement about how to achieve it.

> It's time now... to re-implement the original dream which became this nation... that you and I have the capacity for self-government – the dignity and the ability and the God-given freedom to make our own decisions, to plan our own lives and to control our own destiny.
>
> – from Reagan's campaign speech about "The Creative Society," April 19, 1966

American parents understand the importance of education to their own kids' prospects, and therefore it always ranks as a high priority at election time. Presidents George W. Bush, Bill Clinton, and George H. W. Bush all, at one time or another, have chosen to carry the banner as an "education President." Unfortunately, academic achievement has shown no signs of improvement for all their efforts at increasing education funding.[33] We shouldn't be surprised by the lack of progress. The problem is politicians who only ask "how much?" when they *should* be asking "how?"

Today's public schools – perhaps better labeled "government-run schools" – have no real incentives to respond to the concerns of parents and students. Administrators know that they will get their funding so long as they please the politicians in charge. Kids and their parents don't count as customers; they are just inventory moving through the system. In most cases, they get no say about what school they will attend because it is assigned to them.

If the restaurant industry were configured the same way – assigned customers rather than having to attract them – there is no doubt that costs would rise and quality would

---

[33] Over the past three decades, the United States has drastically increased per-pupil education funding with little evidence of increased achievement. According to the Department of Education, inflation-adjusted education spending grew by 92 percent per pupil between 1972 and 2002, now totaling more than $9,300 per child. (See National Center for Education Statistics, *Digest of Education Statistics*, Table 166, at: http://www.nces.ed.gov/programs/digest/d02/tables/dt166.asp.) Yet that massive spending increase has not yielded results in higher student outcomes. For example, there has been no increase in student performance on the nationally-administrated NAEP exam during the same period. See: http://nces.ed.gov/nationsreportcard/about/trend.asp.)

erode. The diversity of choices would decline as well, since there would be no incentive to serve particular niches that like exotic foods. Is it any wonder that this is exactly what has happened with our government-run schools?

The widespread failure across the American public education system became widely understood during Reagan's first term, when the National Commission of Excellence in Education released *A Nation at Risk*.[34] The report called for an answer to a national emergency: "If an unfriendly foreign power had attempted to impose on America the mediocre educational performance that exists today, we might well have viewed it as an act of war."

Some Presidents would have been tempted to respond with a call for a "war on poor education" and a big increase in public school spending, but Ronald Reagan pointed in the other direction. Addressing the authors of the report in an afternoon speech at the White House, Reagan noted that, according to the report, student achievement had plummeted during the previous two decades – precisely when the federal presence in education became significant.

He outlined a plan to solve America's education crisis by devolving federal authority back to parents and local officials who work at the local level to improve their children's schools. He advocated tuition tax credits, vouchers, and educational savings accounts, arguing that parents ought to have ultimate control over their children's education:

> *I believe that parents, not government, have the primary responsibility for the education of their children. Parental authority is not a right conveyed by*

---

[34] National Commission of Excellence in Education, *A Nation at Risk*, April 1983.

> *the state; rather, parents delegate to their elected school board representatives and State legislators the responsibility for their children's schooling.... Our agenda is to restore quality to education by increasing competition and by strengthening parental choice and local control.[35]*

Unfortunately, none of Reagan's innovations were implemented in the 1980s due to the political realities of the day: a hostile Congress and the increasing political clout of teacher's unions that opposed his reforms. This is tragic because, two decades since Reagan's speech, his diagnosis of the problem appears to have been correct.

Federal spending in K-12 education has doubled, then doubled again – and then again – over the last two decades.[36] Despite these enormous increases, test scores have not budged and a generation of children has slipped through the system, many failing to get even a basic education.[37]

The crisis in public education has not affected families evenly. Wealthy families can afford homes in neighborhoods desirable for their good schools. If those schools don't measure up, many can still afford private alternatives.

---

[35] Reagan, April 26, 1983. Published among The Presidential Papers of Ronald W. Reagan at: http://www.reagan.utexas.edu/resource/speeches/1983/42683d.htm.

[36] The U.S. Department of Education's historical budget tables – available at:http://www.ed.gov/about/overview/budget/history/edhistory.pdf – show that K-12 spending has grown from $6.5 billion in 1983, to $7.3 billion in Reagan's last year in office (1988), to $37.5 billion in 2004.

[37] For example, on the 2003 National Assessment of Educational Progress exam, less than a third of all eighth-graders scored "proficient" in reading or math. A quarter of all students tested scored "below basic" in reading, while a third scored "below basic" in math. For more information, see: http://nces.ed.gov/nationsreportcard.

Reagan's vision for education is one where families of all income classes have the ability to "take their business elsewhere" when choosing a school for their children. When that happens, schools that lose students will have to face up to their problems. It might require actions that are difficult, like firing certain teachers that are doing a poor job or putting resources into making schools safer. But saving our kids from bad educations is worth the costs.

At the same time, some schools will find ways to attract more students, and these innovations will be replicated by others trying to increase their market share. Some people think it is unseemly to use business-speak in education, but competition for customers has generated the improvements we see in the auto industry, computers, telecommunications – improvements we see just about everywhere but education.

Conservatives need to frame the debate as one of individual choice. For too long, teachers' union bosses and their partners in the Democratic Party have acted as though the education system is a jobs program for teachers. In recent years, the teachers unions have become clever in turning their own goals ("find more dues-paying members, no matter if they are qualified to teach") into catch phrases with emotional appeal ("reduce classroom sizes"). But the bottom line is always the same: They want more funding, and they want to deny parents' power to direct their children's education.

The real goal should be giving parents more choices about the best education for their kids. We shouldn't vilify public school teachers – many of whom are heroes trying to make a difference in very difficult situations – but we should question the motives of their union bosses who have the interest of their members, not children, at heart.[38]

In the midst of overall stagnation in education policy, there has been one important positive development. This is that school choice experiments *have* been going on, thanks to the initiatives of certain charities, localities and states. More than 700,000 children attend the nation's 3,000 charter schools – publicly-funded schools that are freed from most bureaucratic rules and are often privately run.[39] Three states have adopted tuition tax credits that help parents pay their child's tuition to private school.

> Americans still believe the American dream. They still yearn for prosperity and still sacrifice so that their children will enjoy it. They mark progress by the level of education reached by members of their families. Parents who never finished high school send their children to college. Each generation stands upon the shoulders of the one before as our nation and our people reach for the stars.
>
> We must keep those dreams alive. We must provide the learning, shape the understanding, and encourage the spirit each generation will need to discover, to create, and to improve the lot of man. But we must also preserve the freedom they will need both to pursue that education and to use it.
>
> – Reagan's speech to the National Catholic Education Association, April 15, 1982.

---

[38] The late Albert Shanker, former head of the American Federation of Teachers, is reported to have said: "If the kids voted and paid dues we would pay attention to them, but they don't vote and they don't pay union dues." (Quoted by Jerry Hume in an address to the Pacific Research Institute, January 30, 2003, see p. 6 at: http://www.pacificresearch.org/pub/sab/educat/speech_hume.pdf.)

[39] "U.S. Charter Schools: History," U.S. Department of Education. Available online at: http://www.uscharterschools.org/pub/uscs_docs/o/history.htm.

Three more have enacted scholarship tax credits that give individuals or businesses a tax break to donate to local charities that provide scholarships to students for private school. In six states, tens of thousands of students are using public scholarship vouchers to attend a private school of their choice.[40] Thousands more attend private school thanks to the generosity of individuals who have reached into their own pockets to fund school choice scholarships. The most recent victories came in 2003, when Governor Bill Owens signed into law Colorado's statewide school voucher program and, in February 2004, when President Bush signed into law Congress's proposal for a school voucher program for low-income students in the nation's capital.

A growing body of research confirms that empowering parents with options boosts parental satisfaction, and there's even some evidence that academic outcomes improve in the presence of school choice.[41]

It's certainly not surprising that giving parents a choice leads to better results and increased satisfaction. After all, parents have a much greater stake in the future of their children than do the politicians and bureaucrats that typically control education decisions. Additionally, school choice defuses some of the most contentious battles in the culture war. Debates about the appropriateness of prayer in school, the teaching of evolution versus creationism, or the

---

[40] *School Choice 2003*, The Heritage Foundation, see: http://www.heritage.org/Research/Education/Schools/loader.cfm?url=/commonspot/security/getfile.cfm&PageID=45087.

[41] For a discussion of the research evidence on school choice, see: Jay Greene, "A Survey of Results from Voucher Experiments: Where We Are and What We Know," Manhattan Institute Civic Report No. 11, July 2000, available online: http://www.manhattan-institute.org/html/cr_11.htm.

role of sexual education disappear if parents are allowed to choose a school that reflects their own moral sensibilities.

Promoting Individual Dignity, Not Dependency

Empowering individuals with more choices and opportunities is also the prescription conservatives should offer for reforming our nation's entitlement programs.

Conservatives care deeply about keeping the public trust and fulfilling promises that have already been made to seniors. We also suggest that safety nets remain in place for the truly impoverished. A third long-term goal, however, is to empower citizens to take greater control of their lives, which includes taking charge of their own retirement savings and medical savings.

Research shows that for what workers currently pay in their FICA taxes – those levies, under the Federal Insurance Contributions Act, that fund old age entitlement programs – they should be able to realize much greater benefits than what Social Security and Medicare promise.[42] And let's not forget that the promises government has made are not sacrosanct. They can be changed by Congress at any time for any reason.

Shouldn't we be looking for ways to let individuals build their own resources so they are not dependent on the government in their later years? In his 1964 "A Time for Choosing" speech, Ronald Reagan noted how Social Security,

---

[42] For a discussion of how individuals could receive greater benefits from a system of private accounts than from Social Security, see Michael Tanner, "The Better Deal: Estimating Rates of Return under a System of Individual Accounts," Cato Project on Social Security Choice Paper No. 31, Cato Institute, October 28, 2003.

because it is structured like a pyramid scheme, cheats most citizens out of dignified retirements:

> *A young man, 21 years of age, working at an average salary – his Social Security contribution would, in the open market, buy him an insurance policy that would guarantee $220 a month at age 65. The government promises $127. He could live it up until he is 31 and then take out a policy that would pay more than Social Security. Now, are we so lacking in business sense that we can't put this program on a sound basis so that people who do require those payments will find that they can get them when they are due – that the cupboard isn't bare? ...At the same time, can't we introduce voluntary features that would permit a citizen who can do better on his own to be excused upon presentation of evidence that he had made provisions for the non-earning years?*[43]

It should not be a surprise that the government is still "lacking in business sense." Over the past 40 years, demographics shifts have made Social Security even less sound. In fact, the whole system is headed toward insolvency. In 2018, the government will be taking in less in taxes than it needs to pay benefits to retirees, so the government will need to raise taxes or cut other programs to meet its obligations to retiring Baby Boomers.[44]

You may wonder about how the Social Security "trust fund" figures into this, but the sad truth is that this has always been an accounting fiction. Your contributions to the trust fund were given away to current beneficiaries, or spent

---

[43] Reagan, "A Time for Choosing," October 27, 1964.
[44] "The 2004 Annual Report of the Board of the Trustees of the Federal Old-Age and Survivors Insurance and Disability Insurance Trust Funds," The Board of Trustees, Federal Old-Age and Survivors Insurance and Disability Insurance Trust Funds, March 23, 2004, p. 8. Available online at: http://www.socialsecurity.gov/OACT/TR/.

on other federal programs, as soon as they came in. In 2018, when the government needs to begin drawing upon the Social Security trust fund, it will need to raise taxes or cut other spending to free up the money to make good on those bonds.[45]

The important principle to understand is that under the existing financing structure, paying the benefits of the next generation of retirees depends entirely on taxing the next generation of workers.

It is critical that Americans consider the nature and magnitude of this problem, so we can put these programs on a fiscally sustainable course. Americans should also embrace the principle that Social Security and Medicare should not create dependency on the government, but instead should fulfill their original purpose and ensure that the elderly enjoy the dignity and independence they have earned.

A well-designed reform plan can do both. While Social Security and Medicare present the greatest challenges facing those of us who want to decrease the size of government in the 21st Century, they also hold the most opportunity for ushering in a new era of personal empowerment and financial autonomy for all Americans.

By allowing current workers to redirect even a small portion of the taxes they currently pay in taxes to a personal retirement account, which would be their private property to be drawn upon during their own retirement, we could begin to pre-fund future benefits and lessen the tax burden on future generations.

---

[45] President's Commission on Social Security, Interim Report, August 2001, pp. 17-19. Available at: http://www.csss.gov/reports/Report-Interim.pdf.

Political opponents say that allowing individuals to put money into private accounts will put retirement savings on the rollercoaster of the stock market. But the main feature of this proposal is that it gives individuals ownership of their own contributions. Even if the personal accounts were invested in government bonds, the rate of return would be higher than what the average American can expect from the current Social Security system. Moreover, it would be inheritable so that someone who paid into the retirement system over their working lives would have a nest egg to pass on.

Conservatives must not shy away from this debate, but instead should take it head on. President Bush's Commission on Social Security has put together a well-designed proposal that gives individuals a choice to put at least a small portion of their Social Security taxes into a personal retirement account, so they are less dependent on the government in old age.[46]

There are tradeoffs to enacting this policy. In order to finance the transition to the funded account, workers who choose to opt out of the current system would receive less in defined benefits. However, the level of benefit reductions would be far less than if we continued with the status quo. Common sense says that it is better to address the problems early. Policymakers must explain the facts, trust the American people to understand, and move forward with this necessary reform.

Our health care system faces many of the same problems as Social Security and the public education system.

---

[46] For background on the President's Commission on Social Security, see: http://www.csss.gov.

Government should step back and figure out how to empower individuals to get the healthcare they need, and how to let their decisions in a free market give direction to health care providers. Then, government could focus on maintaining a sound safety net for the needy, and stop interfering in the doctor-patient relationship.

Like most Americans, you probably have spent time in a doctor's office feeling fairly helpless: kept waiting for long periods, uninformed about treatment options, and suspicious that the doctor is more guided by what our insurance plans will cover than what is in your best interest. It probably makes you wonder why doctors don't treat you like a valued customer.

Well, the answer is that you *aren't* a valued customer. Since health care providers receive their compensation from third-party payers (the health plan you get through your employer, or for older Americans, the Medicare program), they need to satisfy those plans' administrators – not you, the patient.

This creates perverse incentives for just about everyone. In the current system, health insurers cater to the interests of healthier individuals, since they represent a more profitable market than those with expensive medical needs. Doctors cannot focus just on giving an objective analysis of patients' symptoms. They need to consider how their work will be processed by insurance companies. In the meantime, patients with low co-payments tend to over-consume medical services, often wasting doctors' time and leading to higher health care costs.

Wouldn't you like it better if you got a raise equal to what your employer spends on health benefits, and then let you put that (pre-tax) money into a medical savings account? With a medical savings account, you could buy catastrophic insurance in case you face major unanticipated costs, but otherwise pay most medical expenses out of pocket, and hold on to what you don't use.

A large majority of Americans consume less health care than they pay for, when you include the contributions paid by their employers. These individuals all could be building wealth in medical savings accounts for their later years when their expected medical costs will rise. That would free the government to concentrate on helping that smaller portion of the population with special needs.

Unfortunately, public policy debates on health care are trending in the opposite direction. During the 2004 Democratic primary season, nearly every candidate voiced admiration for the kind of "single payer" system that exists in Canada. This is a euphemism for socialized medicine. It's bad enough when an HMO rations your health care or fails to provide choices that you would prefer. It's at least possible to leave your HMO. A single-payer system means that the government rations the care you receive. You could find yourself waiting months for essential procedures, as happens routinely in Canada. Socialized systems inevitably lead to price controls that destroy incentives for new innovations. This is why, for example, Canada has only 1.7 MRI machines for every million individuals, whereas the U.S. ratio is 16 per million. [47]

Davi Harriman MD, William McArthur MD, and Martin Zelder, PhD, "Th availability of Medical Technology in Canada: An International Comparative Study," The Fraser Institute (Vancouver, British Columbia, Canada), 1999.

> Those who've been urging socialized medicine on us for at least two decades have invented a non-existent problem. There isn't a country in the world with government medicine programs that can match what we have in the U.S. Health care here is getting better and better & has been made increasingly available to more & more people. In fact where there are problems they are usually caused by government not by the private practice of medicine."
>
> — from Reagan's radio commentary, "Socialized Medicine I", July 1975 (*In His Own Hand*, p. 365)

It won't be easy to untangle today's very complicated systems of health care financing and health care regulation, but Reagan's words can again help us navigate toward that North Star of individual freedom.

At a bare minimum, conservatives cannot sit by, tongue-tied, as they did during the 2003 debate over adding a prescription drug entitlement to Medicare. The Democrats who drove this debate were not interested in helping low-income seniors get access to pharmaceuticals they cannot afford. What they wanted — and what they got — was an unfunded promise to even the richest older Americans that their prescription drugs will be paid for by younger workers. Is it really fair to take more taxes out of the paycheck of a recent college graduate to subsidize the drug costs of Bill Gates' dad?

A more aggressive approach to the health care debate would see conservatives emphasizing three primary messages: First, that citizens deserve more control over their own health care choices. Second, that America should have the best health care system in the world, which means giving healthcare providers incentives to improve quality and create new innovations via a free market. And finally, that government assistance should be aimed at providing a safety net for the poor, not at making everyone dependent on government bureaucrats for the matters most important to their health.

The Importance of Federalism

One underlying theme throughout this chapter has been about restoring government to its proper role. As we have seen, today's liberals somehow have come to believe that the federal government ought to be the world's biggest pension company and HMO. We know that the real reason for government is to protect our inalienable rights to life, liberty and the pursuit of happiness, as asserted in the Declaration of Independence.

The most essential tasks of government – the ones for which it is uniquely qualified – concern providing for the common defense and establishing relations with foreign powers. These matters are discussed in the next chapter.

But before we leave this discussion of domestic issues, we need to acknowledge that conservatives have stakes in many other policy battles. One way to make progress on several fronts at once is to recognize the larger idea upon which so many of these efforts rest: that is, the restoration of the concept of federalism. And, at the federal level, reasserting a proper separation of powers.

The designers of our Constitution realized that in federalism there's diversity. The Founding Fathers saw the federal system as constructed something like a masonry wall: The States are the bricks, the National Government is the mortar. For the structure to stand plumb with the Constitution, there must be a proper mix of that brick and mortar. Unfortunately, over the years, many people have come increasingly to believe that Washington is the whole wall – a wall that, incidentally, leans, sags, and bulges under its own weight.

– Reagan, speaking to the Annual Convention of the National Conference of State Legislatures in Atlanta, July 30, 1981

Federalism reminds us that the Constitution gave the federal government only limited powers. The Tenth Amendment reads very plainly: "The powers not delegated to the United States by the Constitution, nor prohibited by it to the states, are reserved to the states respectively, or to the people."

The framers of the Constitution realized that America derives great strength from its diversity and that it would be foolish to impose "one-size-fits-all" solutions throughout the country. In fact, one of the great benefits of having states choose their own paths is that they operate as the laboratories of democracy. States can try replicating the programs that produce success in other states, and they can steer clear of those that fail.

One of the better examples of how federalism allows states to find creative solutions to a problem is welfare reform. Reagan recognized this back when he was governor of California in the early 1970s. At that time, the National Governors' Association voted 49-1 in favor of welfare becoming a federal entitlement instead of being left to the states. Reagan was the lone holdout. Reagan was always a skeptic about welfare programs that create incentives for staying destitute. Even more fundamentally, he was adamant the federal government should not encroach on the authority and responsibility of the states.

It seems to me that one of the stultifying effects of [making welfare a federal entitlement] will be to impede, in some cases destroy, the growing and creative work-program efforts being put forth by the private sector. This will stifle ingenuity and freeze failure; and, this is completely out of phase with emerging programs to solve these welfare programs at the local level. It is of deep concern that there are no provisions permitting the states to engage in, or continue, pilot projects which might prove more responsive to state or local needs.

– from Reagan's book, *Sincerely, Ronald Reagan* (1976, p. 52)

Fast forward more than two decades: President Clinton agrees to a Republican Congress' demand to eliminate the federal welfare entitlement and return control to the states. The experience of welfare reform has been very successful, moving millions of individuals out of dependency on government and into productive work. For example, according to Gary Burtless of the Brookings Institution, since reaching a peak in 1994, the number of families collecting cash public assistance for children has dropped more than 3 million – or over 50%.[48]

As with welfare, the fiercest debates in the so-called "culture wars" ought to be resolved at the state or local level, so that laws in a given state more closely reflect the views of its citizens. In many cases, federal courts have over-reached to create "one-size-fits-all" national policies in order to correct "bad laws." But their assigned task is to determine the constitutionality of laws, *not* whether they are bad or good on their merits.

Justice Clarence Thomas made this point in a dissenting opinion in 2003. He said the anti-sodomy law at issue in *Lawrence v. Texas* was "exceedingly silly" and deserved to be repealed, but he voted to uphold the law as Constitutional. The decision to repeal, he argued, is for state legislators representing the people of Texas, not nine unelected Supreme Court justices sitting in Washington, D.C.

Laws involving social mores are bound to generate public disagreement. Among even conservatives, you will find many different ideas about the extent to which the law

---

[48] Gary Burtless, "The Labor Force Status of Mothers Who Are Most Likely to Receive Welfare: Changes Following Reform," *Brookings Web Editorial,* March 30, 2004, http://www.brookings.edu/views/op-ed/burtless/20040330.htm.

should penalize activities – drug use, for example – that are stupid or sinful. What we *should* be able to agree on is that these decisions be made at the state or local level.

When the judicial branch tries to correct the actions of state legislatures, they tend to inflame the cultural wars, rather than put them to rest. Another unfortunate side effect is that these flames have engulfed the nominations process for federal judges, who now are interrogated about their personal views on divisive issues like abortion, rather than their competence and fairness in applying the letter of the law.

How did we get to this sorry state of affairs? With regard to abortion, the *Roe v. Wade* decision of 1973 struck down state restrictions on medical abortions by asserting that a right to privacy exists within the Fourth Amendment of the Constitution (the language of which actually prohibits the government from committing unreasonable searches and seizures).

If the option to have an abortion is widely accepted as a fundamental right, it ought to have been established through the process of amending the Constitution. Likewise, if the public holds that abortion ought to be outlawed entirely, that too should require a Constitutional amendment. Of course, Ronald Reagan – a very passionate opponent of abortion, even writing a book while he was President titled *Abortion and the Conscience of a Nation* – wanted exactly that.

Maybe someday public opinion will be sufficiently pro-life to make such an amendment politically feasible. In the meantime, however, abortion will remain a divisive issue. Restrictions on abortion were becoming less popular around the time of *Roe*, as the feminist movement galvanized support for women being more empowered to choose new roles. As we have learned more about how early fetuses develop human attributes, public opinion about abortion seems to be shifting gradually in the opposite direction.

If the *Roe* decision were struck down, the states would again choose their own ways of answering the troubling ethical questions surrounding abortion. This would be a far more democratic approach than the situation today. Abortion might be entirely outlawed in Alabama, but entirely legal in New York. Most states would wind up in between, reflecting the sensibilities of the community.

Those who are passionately pro-life or passionately pro-choice would appeal to the hearts and minds of the citizens who elect the state legislators. No longer would the Supreme Court decide the issue. Its only opinion on the subject would be that it is not mentioned in the Constitution, and therefore is a subject to be taken up by the states.

By reducing federal involvement in all of these matters, from morality to education to healthcare, individuals will have more control of their lives and government will be able to concentrate on its essential activities. Let's face it, the federal government should not be the messy partisan battlefield that it is today. It should not be a big piñata attracting corporations and interest groups that want favors at the expense of taxpayers.

Rather, the federal government should be dedicated to protecting and defending the American people from terrorists and hostile nations. History handed America the role of protecting and leading the free world during a turbulent 20th Century, and we have entered a new era in which global terrorism is civilization's gravest threat.

To better meet this responsibility – and, as Reagan might have said, keep our "rendezvous with destiny" – we ought to bring the common sense insights of the Founding Fathers back into our domestic politics. We can scale back government to its proper functions and hand future generations a world of greater opportunity, compassion and security.

Chapter 3

Extending the Reagan Vision of a Free World

The past few days when I've been at that window upstairs, I've thought a bit of the 'shining city upon a hill.' The phrase comes from John Winthrop, who wrote it to describe the America he imagined. What he imagined was important because he was an early Pilgrim, an early freedom man. He journeyed here on what today we'd call a little wooden boat; and like the other Pilgrims, he was looking for a home that would be free. I've spoken of the shining city all my political life, but I don't know if I ever quite communicated what I saw when I said it. But in my mind it was a tall, proud city built on rocks stronger than oceans, windswept, God-blessed, and teeming with people of all kinds living in harmony and peace; a city with free ports that hummed with commerce and creativity. And if there had to be city walls, the walls had doors and the doors were open to anyone with the will and the heart to get here. That's how I saw it, and see it still.

And how stands the city on this winter night? More prosperous, more secure, and happier than it was eight years ago. But more than that: After 200 years, two centuries, she still stands strong and true on the granite ridge, and her glow has held steady no matter what storm. And she's still a beacon, still a magnet for all who must have freedom, for all the pilgrims from all the lost places who are hurtling through the darkness, toward home.

— Reagan's "Farewell Address" (Jan 11, 1989)

It may seem counter-intuitive, but we begin this chapter about foreign policy issues with a quote about Ronald Reagan's understanding of America itself.

Reagan's success in bringing the Cold War to a peaceful, victorious conclusion was fueled by an absolute confidence that the United States has an extraordinary, benevolent role to play in the history of mankind. Yet Reagan had no delusion that America is infallible. He believed that America's role as a beacon of freedom created unique responsibilities, not special privileges.

His uncommon vision of America's moral purpose — to advance freedom, human rights, and peace throughout the world — led to significant changes in foreign policy that, in turn, brought about the disintegration of the Soviet empire.

To fulfill Reagan's vision for the future, we need to appreciate the reasons why he believed so strongly in the goodness of the United States. His love of country was not based on attachment to a piece of land, but to a set of principles that has produced history's most successful experiment in liberty. Our nation's founders institutionalized the idea that government derives its authority from the people, who enjoy equality under the law. For the thousands of years before 1776, the destiny of most people was poverty and subservience to a tribal leader, king, or other supreme ruler. The founding of the United States promised that, on these shores, individuals could chart their own destiny.

That's not to say the United States is heaven on earth, as nothing in life comes easy or is guaranteed: Feeding your family requires hard work. Starting a business requires taking financial risks. And creating something new usually requires failing repeatedly before you achieve success. But time and again, free people in America have achieved miraculous results that benefit all of mankind. Life spans have increased, standards of living have skyrocketed, technological innovation has transformed the world, and artists have enriched our lives with incredible new styles of literature, music, and visual arts. Sometimes we take for granted the momentous accomplishments of past generations of Americans. We neglect to ask why other countries have failed to contribute as much as the United States.

We should remember – and communicate to today's young people – that it is no coincidence that the world's most powerful and prosperous country is home to the ideals of freedom. In the Constitution, the United States' founding generation created a near-perfect framework for governance. Our republic preserves lawful order and accommodates changes in government that reflect the will of the people, while allowing for a tremendous amount of individual freedom. Knowing that men – especially politicians – are not angels, the Constitution's signers limited the powers of the federal government and created "checks and balances" to prohibit any single part of the government from growing tyrannical.

Pause for a minute to reflect on this accomplishment. Revolutionaries win power from a despotic king and then, rather than use that power to enrich themselves or gain power over others, they thoughtfully design a system to limit power and protect everyday citizens' rights.

It is true that there are sad chapters in American history. Slavery wounded our nation deeply, with scars that linger even today. The murder and mistreatment of American Indians was reprehensible. Terrible injustices continued well into the 20th Century, tarnishing our national character.

Contemporary Americans should honor those who suffered so dreadfully by pledging to never again allow such violations of human rights on our soil.

Yet while we must never forget the shameful episodes of America's past, we also must remember that, on every continent, history is marked by evil crimes. And it was the logic of the American Declaration of Independence that set in motion a steady increase in freedom and human rights throughout the world.

From the time he was a young boy, Ronald Reagan saw Americans sacrificing their own lives to liberate populations that were oppressed or under siege. He saw that, while Americans failed at times to treat all individuals as equals, its shores always have been a magnet for immigrants seeking opportunity. The obvious implication is that America has been more welcoming than the lands they departed.

Reagan was a master at articulating these basic truths about why America is special among the nations of earth. In his 1964 "A Time for Choosing" speech, just five years after Castro led the communist takeover of Cuba, Ronald Reagan told this story:

> *Not too long ago two friends of mine were talking to a Cuban refugee, a businessman who had escaped from Castro, and in the midst of his story one of my friends turned to the other and said, "We don't know how lucky we are." And the Cuban stopped and said, "How lucky you are? I had someplace to escape to." In that sentence, he told us the entire story. If we lose freedom here, there is no place to escape to. This is the last stand on Earth. And this idea that government is beholden to the people, that it has no other source of power except the sovereign people, is still the newest and most unique idea in all the long history of man's relation to man.*

Younger generations might find it is difficult to grasp just how beleaguered the cause of freedom was during the height of the Cold War, and how much of America had lost its sense of moral leadership until Ronald Reagan reversed the tide of world affairs.

● ● ●

Before Reagan assumed office in 1981, most Americans believed that the Cold War could not be won; that their nation was responsible for many of the world's most difficult problems; and that we should do everything possible to create a stable truce with the communist superpower.

In the 1960s, Lyndon Johnson fought a half-hearted war against communist aggression in Vietnam – not wishing to lose but also afraid to do what was necessary to win. Under Nixon and Ford the United States pursued policies of containment and *detente* to achieve stability among the great powers. Further legitimizing the Soviet empire, Jimmy Carter's Secretary of State, Cyrus Vance, claimed that Carter and Leonid Brezhnev shared "similar dreams and aspirations about the most fundamental issues."[49]

Ronald Reagan had a different perspective. In 1978 – while President Carter pursued a new strategic arms limitation treaty with the Soviets – Reagan told his future National Security Advisor, Richard Allen, "My idea of American policy toward the Soviet Union is simple, and some would say simplistic. It is this: We win and they lose. What do you think of that?"[50]

---

[49] Mona Charen, *Useful Idiots* (New York: Regnery Publishing, Inc., 2003), p 78.
[50] To Richard Allen, quoted in Peter Schweizer, *Reagan's War* (New York: Doubleday. 2002), p. 106

In an ironic sense Karl Marx was right. We are witnessing today a great revolutionary crisis, a crisis where the demands of the economic order are conflicting directly with those of the political order. But the crisis is happening not in the free, non-Marxist West, but in the home of Marxist-Leninism, the Soviet Union. It is the Soviet Union that runs against the tide of history by denying human freedom and human dignity to its citizens. It also is in deep economic difficulty. The rate of growth in the national product has been steadily declining since the fifties and is less than half of what it was then....

The decay of the Soviet experiment should come as no surprise to us. Wherever the comparisons have been made between free and closed societies – West Germany and East Germany, Austria and Czechoslovakia, Malaysia and Vietnam – it is the democratic countries what are prosperous and responsive to the needs of their people. And one of the simple but overwhelming facts of our time is this: Of all the millions of refugees we've seen in the modern world, their flight is always away from, not toward the Communist world. Today on the NATO line, our military forces face east to prevent a possible invasion. On the other side of the line, the Soviet forces also face east to prevent their people from leaving.

The hard evidence of totalitarian rule has caused in mankind an uprising of the intellect and will. Whether it is the growth of the new schools of economics in America or England or the appearance of the so-called new philosophers in France, there is one unifying thread running through the intellectual work of these groups – rejection of the arbitrary power of the state, the refusal to subordinate the rights of the individual to the superstate, the realization that collectivism stifles all the best human impulses.

– Reagan, speaking to Members of the British Parliament,
June 8, 1982

Indeed, Reagan's confident, hawkish perspective would be chastised as simplistic and worse. Before Reagan took office, no place on earth that had "gone communist" had been able to relinquish it, despite uprisings in Hungary (1956), Czechoslovakia (1968), and Poland (1980) that signaled the misery of living in a communist state. This idea that communism, once rooted, was eternal, was known as the Brezhnev Doctrine.

It would not survive the Reagan presidency. Indeed, after Reagan was inaugurated, communist insurgents would fail to gain another inch of ground, and more rapidly than anyone would have predicted (save, perhaps, Reagan himself), the entire evil empire crumbled away. In hindsight, it is apparent how correct Reagan was to see beyond America's temporary loss of confidence at the end of 1970s. He was certain that all people yearn for freedom and that America remained a beacon of hope to those who struggle against tyranny. He believed that when America acts weak, despotic regimes are encouraged to be more belligerent. When America is strong, it can thwart the ambitions of such governments. He also believed that the Soviet system was inherently unstable because it depended on the cooperation of an oppressed population.

Reagan's courageous and inventive approach to weakening the Soviet Union and winning the Cold War is well-documented in books such as *Reagan's War* by Peter Schweizer. Since we are concentrating here on lessons that will be applicable to future generations of conservatives, we will skip the nuances of this history and concentrate on a few big ideas that are broadly applicable to foreign affairs – and especially the current climate as the United States faces the threat of global terror and the states that enable it.

Perhaps the most important principle is the moral clarity Reagan brought to international affairs. Reagan identified the Soviet Union as "the locus of evil in the modern world."[51] He knew an outcry would follow from those whose careers were invested in maintaining diplomatic niceties or who believed that accommodating the Soviet Union was the only

---

[51] Ronald Reagan, "Remarks at the Annual Convention of the National Association of Evangelicals," March 8, 1983.

strategy left to the United States. But Reagan also knew it was the truth, and the truth has a funny way of winning arguments over time.

Communism survived through fear. Lenin and Stalin massacred huge numbers of their countrymen to subdue the population into compliance with the communist leadership. It is estimated that some 20 million people died from Soviet atrocities: an average of more than 5,000 (in other words, more casualties than we suffered on September 11) for *each week* of the USSR's 74-year existence.[52]

After World War II, war-weary leaders in the West feared confronting the Soviet Union as it brought satellite countries under its control and fomented communist revolution in the developing world. As the years rolled on, foreign policy discussion came to embrace obvious double-standards that countenanced horrible crimes by communist governments. Political leaders who built careers as "anti-anti-communists" (i.e., people who, reacting against the bullying style of Joe McCarthy, came to believe all anti-communists were alarmists) feared facing up to their complicity in apologizing for evil dictatorships.

From the beginning of his political career, Reagan made a habit of reminding people of uncontestable facts that demonstrated the United States' benevolence on the world stage and the Soviet Union's belligerence.

---

[52] Stephane Courtois, et al., *The Black Book of Communism: Crimes, Terror, Repression*: Harvard University Press (Cambridge, MA, 1999).

[53] "The Image of America and the Youth of the World, with Sen. Robert F. Kennedy and Gov. Ronald Reagan," was broadcast over the CBS Television Network and the CBS Radio Network, Monday, May 15, 1967. A transcript of the broadcast appears at: http://www.cs.umb.edu/jfklibrary/rfk-reag.htm.

For instance, in 1967, Reagan debated Robert Kennedy in a CBS broadcast organized like a town hall meeting.[53] When the subject of normalizing relations with the Soviet Union and China came up, Reagan (foreshadowing a statement he'd make in more dramatic fashion 20 years later) proposed that a good first step would be "if the Berlin Wall should disappear." How could people consider the Soviets as morally equivalent to the United States when it had to imprison entire populations to sustain its empire?

Here are examples of other simple truths that many tried to overlook, but Reagan forced the world to recognize:

- The United States has never sought an empire – *"Historians looking back at our time will note the consistent restraint and peaceful intentions of the West. They will note that it was the democracies who refused to use the threat of their nuclear monopoly in the forties and early fifties for territorial or imperial gain. Had that nuclear monopoly been in the hands of the Communist world, the map of Europe – indeed, the world – would look very different today."*[54]

- It is reckless to put faith in treaties that will not be honored by the other party – *"...As good Marxist-Leninists, the Soviet leaders have openly and publicly declared that the only morality they recognize is that which will further their cause, which is world revolution... [According to their guiding sprit, Vladimir Lenin,] morality is entirely subordinate to the interests of class war. And everything is moral that is necessary for the annihilation of the old, exploiting social order and for uniting the proletariat... Well, I*

---

[54] Ronald Reagan, "Address to Members of the British Parliament," July 8, 1982.

> *think the refusal of many influential people to accept this elementary fact of Soviet doctrine illustrates an historical reluctance to see totalitarian powers for what they are."*[55]

- Mass immigrations always are toward freer societies — *"One of the simple but overwhelming facts of our time is this: Of all the millions of refugees we've seen in the modern world, their flight is always away from, not toward the Communist world. Today on the NATO line, our military forces face east to prevent a possible invasion. On the other side of the line, the Soviet forces also face east to prevent their people from leaving."*[56]

From these truths, and the moral confidence Reagan had in the goodness of America, came the Reagan doctrine of rebuilding America's military might so that the United States could, cautiously but effectively, confront communist aggression and further the cause of freedom and human rights.

The guiding principles of Reagan's foreign policy were clear from the beginning of his administration. His first inaugural address, part of which is reprinted below, explained clearly that America's goal is peace, but that attaining and preserving peace requires strength and resolve to stand with allies in the brotherhood of free nations.

---

[55] Ronald Reagan, "Remarks at the Annual Convention of the National Association of Evangelicals," March 8, 1983.
[56] Ronald Reagan, "Address to Members of the British Parliament," July 8, 1982.

I believe we, the Americans of today, are ready to act worthy of ourselves, ready to do what must be done to ensure happiness and liberty for ourselves, our children and our children's children.

And as we renew ourselves here in our own land, we will be seen as having greater strength throughout the world. We will again be the exemplar of freedom and a beacon of hope for those who do not now have freedom.

To those neighbors and allies who share our freedom, we will strengthen our historic ties and assure them of our support and firm commitment. We will match loyalty with loyalty. We will strive for mutually beneficial relations. We will not use our friendship to impose on their sovereignty, for our own sovereignty is not for sale.

As for the enemies of freedom, those who are potential adversaries, they will be reminded that peace is the highest aspiration of the American people. We will negotiate for it, sacrifice for it; we will not surrender for it—now or ever.

Our forbearance should never be misunderstood. Our reluctance for conflict should not be misjudged as a failure of will. When action is required to preserve our national security, we will act. We will maintain sufficient strength to prevail if need be, knowing that if we do so we have the best chance of never having to use that strength.

Above all, we must realize that no arsenal, or no weapon in the arsenals of the world, is so formidable as the will and moral courage of free men and women. It is a weapon our adversaries in today's world do not have. It is a weapon that we as Americans do have. Let that be understood by those who practice terrorism and prey upon their neighbors.

– Reagan's Inaugural Address, January 20, 1981

Peace Through Strength

In 1981, Reagan inherited a military that was demoralized and falling behind in the arms race. Reagan prioritized rebuilding U.S. military prowess above all else.

Critics believed that this arms buildup made the catastrophe of nuclear war more likely. Reagan countered, "Nations do not distrust each other because they are armed;

they are armed because they distrust each other."[57]   He believed that the U.S. military could be a force for good in the world, just as when it helped liberate Europe from the Nazis. American strength would temper the ambitions of aggressors, and could actually contribute to building trust when other nations observe that the United States is not interested in exploiting its overwhelming power for selfish purposes.

While some have lamented the leadership role that comes with American power, most Americans share Reagan's belief that maintaining our military superiority will help achieve a more peaceful world.

An important part of maintaining this advantage and protecting Americans from aggression involves thinking creatively about how security threats continue to evolve. One of Reagan's most inspired moves as President was the launching of the "strategic defense initiative" to develop a shield against the nuclear missiles that the Soviet Union had aimed at U.S. cities. He saw that technological advances could transform the Cold War stalemate of "mutual assured destruction" under which the United States could avenge – but not prevent – a first strike against it.

The anti-missile technology Reagan envisioned is now expected to be deployed, at least in a limited version, by the end of 2004. Not a moment too soon, given North Korea's attempts to use their nuclear missiles to blackmail the United States and the likelihood that other hostile nations are pursuing nuclear capabilities.

---

[57] Ronald Reagan, "Speech to the Students of Moscow University," May 31, 1988.

Other advances in military technology are enabling the United States to fight more effectively, targeting specific threats and limiting the deaths of non-combatants. War will always involve tragedies, but as George W. Bush said after the end of major combat operations in Iraq, "It is a great moral advance when the guilty have far more to fear from war than the innocent."[58]

Of course, in the current climate where terrorism is the major security threat, intelligence gathering is of paramount importance. Reagan thought that scrutiny of the FBI and CIA for potential abuses was constructive, but only to a point. He worried in the 1970s that Americans were asleep to the real threat of hostile foreign powers because of heightened sensitivities with regard to civil liberties. "Isn't it time for someone to ask if we aren't threatened more by the people the FBI and CIA are watching than we are by the FBI and the CIA?"[59]

When running for President, Reagan stressed the crucial role of intelligence:

> *We must once again restore the United States intelligence community. A Democratic Congress, aided and abetted by the Carter administration, has succeeded in shackling and demoralizing our intelligence services to the point that they no longer function effectively as a component part of our defenses. With all the military and terrorist threats confronting us, we need a first-class intelligence capability, with high morale and dedicated people.*[60]

---

[58] George W. Bush, "Remarks from the USS Abraham Lincoln At Sea Off the Coast of San Diego, California," May 1, 2003. See: http://www.whitehouse.gov/news/releases/2003/05/iraq/20030501-15.html.

[59] Ronald Reagan, "Intelligence," radio commentary of June 15, 1977, collected in *Reagan In His Own Hand*, p. 125.

[60] Ronald Reagan, "Campaign Speech to Chicago Council on Foreign Relations," March 13, 1980, collected in *Reagan in His Own Hand*, p. 476.

Investing smartly to preserve the country's security and keeping Americans resolute to defeat the threat of international terrorism are essential tasks for the foreseeable future.

Of course, we must be extremely reticent to use our military power. As much as possible, we must keep our soldiers, and the inevitable innocent victims of war, out of harm's way. Each commitment that America makes spreads thin our military capacities – best to save our strength for only those situations essential to national security.

> Our experience in Lebanon led to the adoption by the administration of a set of principles to guide America in the application of military force abroad, and I would recommend it to future presidents. The policy we adopted included these principles:
>
> 1. The United States should not commit its forces to military action overseas unless the cause is vital to our national interest.
>
> 2. If the decision is made to commit our forces to combat abroad, it must be done with the clear intent and support needed to win. It should not be a halfway or tentative commitment, and there must be clearly defined and realistic objectives.
>
> 3. Before we commit our troops to combat, there must be reasonable assurance that the cause we are fighting for and the actions we take will have the support of the American people and Congress. (We all felt that the Vietnam War had turned into such a tragedy because military action had been undertaken without sufficient assurances that the American people were behind it.)
>
> 4. Even after all these other tests are met, our troops should be committed to combat abroad *only* as a last resort, when no other choice is available.
>
> – Ronald Reagan, *An American Life*, p. 466

Further, any foreign intervention is bound to create unintended consequences. Remember that the 1991 Gulf War accomplished its strategic objective of removing Iraq from Kuwait, but it entailed creating a military presence in Saudi Arabia that Osama bin Laden later used as a grievance to develop his anti-American terrorist network.

This likelihood – that war always has unexpected results, many of which are negative – ought to bias leaders against military adventures, especially when no vital national interests are at stake. But this warning should not create paralysis. When circumstances require assuming risks and confronting dangers, the U.S. military should have our full support to achieve victory.

Reagan was profoundly affected by the failure of Johnson and then Nixon to achieve victory in Vietnam. Speaking to a group of students on April 26, 1973, he said:

> *Never again must this country ask a young man to fight and die unless it's for something we believe in so much that we tell him at the same time "we're going to turn our full energies behind you to get it over with and to win it."* [61]

Given the capacity of the American people to produce the wealth necessary to achieve military superiority and the heroism of American soldiers through our history, Reagan believed Americans should be able to win any conflict we find necessary to fight – provided we have the resolve to commit to victory.

The Brotherhood of Free Nations

Having the strength and resolve to secure our national interests begins with building and maintaining firms alliances with countries friendly to freedom.

Reagan began his administration pledging to stand strong beside America's loyal allies and reminding the free

---

[61] Peter D. Hannaford, *The Quotable Ronald Reagan* (New York: Regnery Publishing, Inc., 1999), p. 181.

nations of the world of their common values and common destiny. Reagan's celebrated speech at Pointe du Hoc, France, on the 40th anniversary of D-Day, made this point to our European allies whose determination to stand up to the Soviets was wavering:

> *We are bound today by what bound us 40 years ago, the same loyalties, traditions, and beliefs. We're bound by reality. The strength of America's allies is vital to the United States, and the American security guarantee is essential to the continued freedom of Europe's democracies. We were with you then; we are with you now. Your hopes are our hopes, and your destiny is our destiny.*[62]

Americans have always seen the importance of winning the loyalty and respect of other nations that aspire to peace and value individual rights. But coalition building cannot be an end in itself. Reagan understood there are times that America must show leadership and look after its interests, alone if need be.

For example, many during Reagan's era supported a "nuclear freeze" that would have played to the Soviet Union's advantage. Strongly influenced by books such as *The Treaty Trap* by Laurene Beilenson[63] – which distinguished between "the paper world of making treaties" and "the real would of performing them" – Reagan refused to be party to treaties that rewarded intransigence or put false faith in the promises

---

[62] Ronald Reagan, "Remarks Commemorating the 40th Anniversary of the Normandy Invasion," June 6, 1984. Available online at: http://www.reagan.utexas.edu/resource/speeches/1984/60684a.htm.

[63] The influence of Laurene Beilenson's work on Reagan's thinking is discussed in Kiron K. Skinner, Annelise Anderson, Martin Anderson (eds.), *Reagan: In His Own Hand* (New York: Simon & Schuster, 2001), p. 48.

of tyrannical governments. When he finally achieved the historic Intermediate Nuclear Force (INF) Treaty in 1987, after years of strengthening his hand and refusing to be bullied in negotiations with Gorbachev, Reagan was the one dictating the terms and setting the tone.

In recent years, foreign policy debate has revolved around the extent to which the United States ought to defer to the United Nations. Reagan addressed this issue in some of the radio commentaries he wrote in the 1970s, pointing out the organization's history of failure in preserving the peace and protecting fundamental human rights.[64]

Since September 11, we have seen more evidence that the United Nations is dysfunctional, riddled with conflicts of interest, and unable to enforce its own resolutions. The idea that the United Nations represents the conscience of the world's peoples is false; rather, it is an association of world governments, many of them unelected and despotic. During the Iraq War in 2003, the U.N. Human Rights Commission was chaired by Libya and included five other nations considered among the world's most repressive regimes. At about the same time, we discovered that the U.N.'s Oil for Food program was exploited by Saddam's Baathist regime to fund the construction of palaces, while the U.N. bureaucracy had reaped billions of dollars by implementing this program – no wonder the U.N.'s leadership was so opposed to upsetting the status quo in Iraq.

This is not to say that the case for attacking Iraq was clear-cut; reasonable minds can certainly differ on the merits. But the critics who suggest that foreign policy decisions are illegitimate unless approved by the United Nations are

---

[64] Ronald Reagan, "United Nations," radio commentary of May 1975, collected in *Reagan In His Own Hand*, p. 159.

sacrificing our sovereignty to leaders from China, France, Russia, and the United Kingdom whom we did not elect. Americans must recognize that envy and narrow interests will at times put other countries at odds with the United States.

The best way to meet the twin goals of protecting American security and winning allies in the brotherhood of free nations is to practice a Reaganite foreign policy – and to preach it.

By speaking boldly on the world stage about the moral purpose of America, other countries of the world – even those that currently harbor anti-American resentments – eventually will understand our sincere hope that the rest of the world enjoys the human rights, peace and prosperity that have blessed our own land for so long.

> I've been reflecting on what the past eight years have meant and mean. And the image that comes to mind like a refrain is a nautical one – a small story about a big ship, and a refugee and a sailor. It was back in the early eighties, at the height of the boat people. And the sailor was hard at work on the carrier Midway, which was patrolling the South China Sea. The sailor, like most American servicemen, was young, smart, and fiercely observant. The crew spied on the horizon a leaky little boat. And crammed inside were refugees from Indochina hoping to get to America. The Midway sent a small launch to bring them to the ship and safety. As the refugees made their way through the choppy seas, one spied the sailor on deck and stood up and called out to him. He yelled, "Hello, American sailor. Hello, freedom man." A small moment with a big meaning, a moment the sailor, who wrote it in a letter, couldn't get out of his mind. And when I saw it, neither could I. Because that's what it was to be an American in the 1980s. We stood, again, for freedom. I know we always have, but in the past few years the world again – and in a way, we ourselves – rediscovered it.
>
> – Reagan's farewell address, January 11, 1989

We can champion worthy causes that improve living standards and remove terrible threats. For instance,

President Bush rightly identified the AIDS plague sweeping Africa, where approximately 30 million are now infected, as a cause America cannot ignore. Of course, humanitarian actions like this need to be managed carefully. Simply offering foreign aid by writing large checks has arguably hurt developing countries more than it has helped. Too often, aid sent for humanitarian purposes has propped up corrupt, socialist regimes – in doing so, generous Americans have unwittingly strengthened the root cause of poverty, instead of diminishing it.

In unfree parts of the world, we can again be on the right side of history and forge a more lasting peace by giving moral encouragement to brave dissidents and reformers who carry the torch of freedom. In Peggy Noonan's *When Character Was King*, we read of how dissidents in the Soviet Union found hope in Reagan's tough talk. One veteran of the Soviet gulag, Anatoly Shcharansky, released due to pressure from the Reagan administration, was able to thank Reagan in person. "I told him that his speech about the Evil Empire was a great encourager for us. An American leader was calling a spade a spade – he understood the nature of the Soviet Union."[65]

In addition to challenging brutal regimes, the long-term quest for world peace hinges on bringing more nations – now on the fence between freedom and oppression – into the family of modern nations.

Reagan saw that ideological rivalry and nationalistic prejudice thrive in climates of ignorance and fear. He wished that world leaders who saw the United States as a threat or

---

[65] Peggy Noonan, *When Character Was King* (New York: Viking Press, 2001), p. 214.

enemy could visit and observe the simple decency of American life. Today, our challenge remains the same. The world's dangerous nations are those most isolated from the world: North Korea, Syria, Iran, Cuba.

> I only wish I could get in a helicopter with Gorbachev and fly over the United States. And I would ask him to point to people's homes, and we could stop at some of them. Then he would see how Americans live, in clean and lovely homes, with a second car or a boat in the driveway. If I can just get through to him about the difference between our two systems, I really think we could see big changes in the Soviet Union.
>
> – Reagan in 1985, as quoted in Dinesh D'Souza's *Ronald Reagan: How an Ordinary Man Became an Extraordinary Leader*, p. 1.

The prospects for peace are bolstered when there is close contact among countries via cultural exchange or trades of goods and services. One of the reasons to be optimistic about the process of globalization is the way that new relationships between trading partners tend to wipe away old disputes. When countries want to attract tourists and benefit from trade and foreign investment, there is less incentive to get caught in petty hostilities and a much greater incentive to maximize stability. Free trade between nations creates prosperity and opportunity, and undermines the alienation that breeds violence and extremism.

Fostering peace and greater individual freedom is one of the least appreciated effects of free trade. It is well known that free trade yields huge economic benefits to consumers (which, overall, outweigh the pain of job losses in some sectors – an inevitable feature of a dynamic capitalist economy). When President Clinton joined Republicans in Congress to enact the North American Free Trade Agreement (NAFTA), a dramatic increase in trade resulted, while unemployment remained very low.

A less understood benefit of NAFTA was the increases in economic activity helped Mexicans achieve greater political rights. Mexico had one of the most backward political systems in the world throughout the 20th Century, dominated by the PRI party for 71 years. But this one-party reign came to an end with the election of Vicente Fox in 2000. A key factor in Fox's rise was the success of NAFTA in creating vibrant centers of commerce separate from communities where the PRI party dominated. As more Mexican citizens became middle-class – and therefore not reliant upon favors from entrenched political cronies – true competition arrived in Mexico's political scene.

So two big ideas go hand-in-hand: Countries that are free, tend to be friendly. And countries that are trading with the outside world, tend to be free.

No wonder living conditions are so miserable in unfree countries. While we might assume that all leaders must desire the improvement of their people's fortunes, it has been demonstrated that political leaders stay in power longer when they preside over terrible economies.[66] When there is little wealth in a country, ruling dictators hold essentially all the cards. They can use what wealth does exist to buy the loyalty of others in the country, and to punish those that threaten their power. By limiting the opportunity of the people to get ahead except by serving the state, dictators enhance their own power at the expense of the citizenry.

Ronald Reagan saw the strategic necessity of extending the promise of capitalism, asserting his moral vision of America,

---

[66] Bruce Bueno de Mesquita and Hilton L. Root, "The Political Roots of Poverty: The Economic Logic of Autocracy" (*The National Interest*, Summer 2002, pp. 27-37).

and converting more countries to freedom. Winning the hearts and minds of the world's people was especially salient as the world's other superpower was trying to foment revolution and impose communism on nations all over the globe.

And this project has special relevance again, as the United States confronts another extremist ideology that preys on those who lack other prospects for advancement and self-realization, and therefore are prone to fanaticism.

> Effective antiterrorist action has also been thwarted by the claim that – as the quip goes – "One man's terrorist is another man's freedom fighter." That's a catchy phrase, but also misleading. Freedom fighters do not need to terrorize a population into submission. Freedom fighters target the military forces and the organized instruments of repression keeping dictatorial regimes in power. Freedom fighters struggle to liberate their citizens from oppression and to establish a form of government that reflects the will of the people. Now, this is not to say that those who are fighting for freedom are perfect or that we should ignore problems arising from passion and conflict. Nevertheless, one has to be blind, ignorant, or simply unwilling to see the truth if he or she is unable to distinguish between those I just described and terrorists. Terrorists intentionally kill or maim unarmed civilians, often women and children, often third parties who are not in any way part of a dictatorial regime. Terrorists are always the enemies of democracy.
>
> – Reagan, Radio Address on Terrorism, May 31, 1986

The Challenge in 2004

The Cold War is over. But the free world again faces a global threat in the terrorism of radical Islamists.

While the challenge is different from the one Reagan confronted, the essential principles that guided his thinking remain applicable today.

- Take inspiration from a moral vision of America: extending freedom and opportunity, and confronting those that wish evil upon innocents.

- Support our troops; invest in what our military and intelligence services need to face a new kind of enemy; use our greatest asset – the imagination and determination of free people – to solve the problems that confront us.

- Build and nurture alliances, but not at the cost of losing sight of our security goals.

- Hold all countries to the same standard of human rights, and encourage movement in the direction of a free society.

Of course, putting these principles into practice will never be simple. At times – often, even – the principles conflict with one another, and judgment needs to be exercised on a case by case basis.

For instance, Reagan's decision to pull U.S. forces out of Lebanon shortly after the 1982 attack that killed 282 marines can be seen as yielding to terrorism and thereby encouraging more of it. At the same time, if he'd chosen another course, Reagan may have unnecessarily put American lives at risk in a situation judged to be of lesser strategic importance.

The War on Terror involves difficult trade-offs, especially between security and liberty. In our opinion, the currently controversial Patriot Act has been a positive step in waging this war and preventing, thus far, another major attack on U.S. soil. But we are also happy to see vocal critics of the Patriot Act serving as watchdogs, ready to cause a public outcry if the government violates civil liberties. Intense public discussion of these matters is crucial for identifying gross abuses of power, or lapses in protecting the public.

The coming years will bring new international dilemmas and, with them, difficult decisions.

One thing is certain. Ronald Reagan would be hopeful about the big picture of what the United States has embarked upon, challenging those who carry out barbaric attacks for evil or misguided reasons and extending the American promise of freedom, tolerance, and compassion to places where these virtues have no recent tradition.

• • •

As Americans rise to meet this new challenge, what inspiration can be drawn from President Reagan?

Historians will record that, to use Margaret Thatcher's words, Ronald Reagan "won the Cold War without firing a shot." Reagan's foreign policy marked a sharp break in foreign policy during the Cold War. He strengthened American capabilities, weakened those of our adversaries, and toughened the resolve a nation that had begun to doubt its role as a global beacon of freedom.

And, most important, he restored idealism to the heart of the American experience. He reminded us of the central lessons of history, and asserted America's destiny in creating a more peaceful world.

On June 7, 1987, standing at the Brandenburg Gate, with the Berlin Wall behind him, Reagan addressed a crowd of West Berliners and issued a challenge to the Soviet Union. The communist leaders of East Berlin blasted music on their side of the wall to try to prevent the speech from being heard by their own citizens. Reagan spoke, undeterred:

> *In the 1950s, Khrushchev predicted: 'We will bury you.' But in the West today, we see a free world that has achieved a level of prosperity and well-being unprecedented in all human history. In the Communist world, we see failure, technological backwardness, declining standards of health, even want of the most*

basic kind – too little food. Even today, the Soviet Union still cannot feed itself. After these four decades, then, there stands before the entire world one great and inescapable conclusion: Freedom leads to prosperity. Freedom replaces the ancient hatreds among the nations with comity and peace. Freedom is the victor.

And now the Soviets themselves may, in a limited way, be coming to understand the importance of freedom. We hear much from Moscow about a new policy of reform and openness. Some political prisoners have been released. Certain foreign news broadcasts are no longer being jammed. Some economic enterprises have been permitted to operate with greater freedom from state control.

Are these the beginnings of profound changes in the Soviet state? Or are they token gestures, intended to raise false hopes in the West, or to strengthen the Soviet system without changing it? We welcome change and openness; for we believe that freedom and security go together, that the advance of human liberty can only strengthen the cause of world peace. There is one sign the Soviets can make that would be unmistakable, that would advance dramatically the cause of freedom and peace.

General Secretary Gorbachev, if you seek peace, if you seek prosperity for the Soviet Union and Eastern Europe, if you seek liberalization: Come here to this gate! Mr. Gorbachev, open this gate! Mr. Gorbachev, tear down this wall!

On November 9, 1989 – two years and five months after Reagan issued his challenge – the Berlin Wall fell.

In September of the following year, Ronald Reagan, now retired from his duties in the Oval Office, returned to Russia and the former Eastern Bloc to see the march of freedom with his own eyes.

In Moscow, Reagan marveled at the transformation toward greater freedom.

In Poland, he was given a sword by Lech Welesa's parish priest, who said: "I am giving you the saber for helping us to chop off the head of communism." A cheering crowd of 7,000 sang "Sto Lat (May He Live 100 Years)," traditionally reserved for the only most popular Polish leaders.

In Berlin, Reagan returned to see the "scar of a wall" that had divided a continent between free and unfree. Now in ruins, it was an artifact from a vanishing past. Sabine Bergmann-Pohl, the President of the East German Parliament, would remark: "Mr. President, we have much to thank you for." As Reagan walked through Brandenburg Gate with the mayors of East and West Berlin, stoneworkers paused from their preparations for the coming month's German unification ceremony. They waved and cheered from the scaffolding. People lined Reagan's path as he made his way to the remnant of the wall, where he'd take a hammer and chisel to the symbol of the bygone era. "Ronnie, we love you! There would never be a free Germany without you!" one Berlin man shouted as Reagan walked forward.[67]

Reagan must felt have felt enormous satisfaction. Defeating communism had been his life's work. This tour of liberated countries would be reported on as a "victory tour" – and certainly Reagan deserved one. But in the details of these media accounts, we can glimpse that Reagan remained thoughtful, determined, not a bit complacent. "I'm glad the wall is gone," he remarked to celebrating Germans, "but you

---

[67] Jonathan Kaufman, "A Reagan wish fulfilled; He returns to Berlin and finds the wall has indeed been torn down," *The Boston Globe*, September 13, 1990, p. 2.

can't be happy before the whole world knows the freedom you have here."[68]

Let's take these words to heart. Our challenge is continue spreading freedom across the globe, and – make no mistake – we all have important roles to play.

---

[68] Alan Ferguson, "Happy Reagan celebrates fall of Berlin Wall," *The Toronto Star*, September 13, 1990, p. A2.

Chapter 4

Our Rendezvous with Destiny

In the preceding pages we've considered how President Reagan guided a political revolution that gave birth to greater opportunity and prosperity here in America, and a new dawn of freedom across the globe. Reagan's vision for domestic and economic policy unleashed an 18-year economic boom that brought unprecedented levels of prosperity to American society. Reagan's vision of international affairs led to victory in the Cold War, and the end of a Soviet empire responsible for the deaths of more than 20 million people throughout the 20th Century.

Of course, there is still much work to be done to spread greater freedom and prosperity both in America and across the globe. But we cannot underestimate the debt we owe to Reagan for achieving so much. A first small step to paying that debt is to commit ourselves to finishing the Reagan Revolution.

This book is being published in advance of the 2004 elections, which provide the American people with a new "time for choosing." But no matter whether George Bush or John Kerry ends up in the White House next year, conservatives will need to continue to work hard to build a consensus around a Reaganite vision. There is no short cut. This project will continue for decades to come.

> Just then there was a quiet knock on the door of our cabin and I was reminded that we were taking our last ride aboard what had been Air Force One. We were told there was a gathering of all those on board — staff, press, and Secret Service — a chance to say good-bye before we landed. There were warm handshakes, tearful embraces, and lots of picture taking. Finally, champagne was poured and glasses were raised. "Mission accomplished, Mr. President," someone called out, "Mission accomplished." Not yet, I thought to myself, not yet.
>
> — closing words of Reagan's autobiography, *An American Life*, p. 726.

Thomas Jefferson wrote that, "The natural progress of things is for liberty to yield and government to gain ground." Irish politician and judge John Philpot Curran gave us the quote, "The price of liberty is eternal vigilance." All of us should commit ourselves to the difficult task of protecting and advancing liberty. The example of Ronald Reagan shows how much can be accomplished by one man speaking the truth and sticking to his principles. If millions of us put our energy into the long-term project of advancing conservative ideas, policy victories will soon come and then we will witness brighter prospects in our country and throughout the world.

This final chapter considers how we can all make a difference in preserving and extending the freedoms that took root in this nation. It is a difficult but important task — one that Reagan himself assigned to us in his farewell address from the Oval Office:

Finally, there is a great tradition of warnings in presidential farewells, and I've got one that's been on my mind for some time. But oddly enough it starts with

one of the things I'm proudest of in the past eight years:
the resurgence of national pride that I called the new
patriotism. This national feeling is good, but it won't
count for much, and it won't last unless it's grounded in
thoughtfulness and knowledge. An informed patriotism
is what we want.... We've got to do a better job of getting
across that America is freedom–freedom of speech,
freedom of religion, freedom of enterprise. And freedom
is special and rare. It's fragile; it needs protection.

So how do we achieve this goal over the long-term, so
that future generations understand and appreciate freedom
as the basis of America's great heritage?

One thing is for sure: It's not as simple as getting up on
Election Day and voting for candidates with "R"s next to their
names. Blind loyalty to any particular political party means
it will start taking your vote for granted. It's far more
important to be loyal to the essential, enduring principles
that we have identified in the preceding chapters.

Reagan, of course, first became involved in campaigns
as a Democrat. When asked why he left the Democratic Party,
Reagan would say, "The Democratic Party left me."

So let's agree on a couple ideas right off the bat. First, it
is within our power to make sure that the Republican Party
does a better job of standing up for Reaganite principles and
putting them into action. Second, when political candidates
of any party adopt the mantle of Ronald Reagan and
demonstrate a commitment to conservative ideas – even when
the going gets rough for them – let's pledge our enthusiastic
support. But even then, remember that there's a lot more to
this project than just the political battlefield.

In real wars, physical combat is only the most visible
aspect of a complex, multi-layered operation. Recruiting,
training, positioning, intelligence gathering, building supply

lines – all of these have more to do with the success of a military operation than the battlefield heroism of any single soldier.

So too with the war of ideas. We were incredibly fortunate to have a man like Ronald Reagan carry the conservative torch during a critical moment in history. Who knows if we'll have such luck again? If the conservative movement is to succeed, we need to work hard on all the other aspects, so the cause does not depend on a future Reagan fortuitously emerging.

If we work hard to make sure conservative ideas get a fair hearing, if we stay involved with our communities and specific policy battles, if we think carefully about what causes to support with our money and time – we can ensure that future generations of Americans will know the blessings of liberty.

Only a minority of Americans get involved in projects concerning the future direction of policy and ideas. There is a concept called "rational ignorance" that explains why it is perfectly logical for people to *not* vote and *not* stay informed. After all, one vote is exceedingly unlikely to alter the outcome of any election, so why bother?

The flipside of this concept is actually encouraging. Those of us who do put real effort into staying informed and promoting our ideas can have a huge impact. If our efforts can combine to motivate a few million voters to be more involved, informed, and principled, then we will have created a block of voters that can shift the outcome of elections in the right direction.

There would be further ripple effects: Our new principled conservative voters will exert a powerful effect on others who remain "rationally ignorant." Think of how many people don't have firm ideas about politics, but have enough of a caricatured perspective of conservatives to make them vote for Democrats. If a sizable number of us become spokespeople and activists for the ideas we believe in, we will be much better able to demonstrate the true nature of conservatism – respecting individual rights, enabling economic advancement, and promoting equality under the law. Even people who don't fully embrace our policy recommendations will have a better understanding and respect for the conservative movement.

Of course, none of this will happen overnight. There tend to be long periods of time when it's very difficult to change the status quo. Changes in the intellectual climate typically occur in reaction to unexpected events, and the course of history depends on, as Milton Friedman has suggested, what ideas are on the shelf at the time.[69]

When the Great Depression struck at the end of the 1920's, the public came to accept an explanation that the situation was the fault of unrestrained capitalism. Economists like Friedman have since shown that bad government decisions – mostly mistakes by the Federal Reserve and protectionist trade policy – were the real culprit that turned the bursting of that earlier stock market bubble into a decade-long nightmare. Unfortunately, these ideas were not "on the shelf" of most opinion leaders at the time, and a generation of Americans came to believe that big government spending programs would help the economy.

---

[69] Author's notes from Milton Friedman's address to the Mont Pelerin Society, Regional Meeting, Vancouver, British Columbia, Canada, August 30, 1999.

September 11, 2001, was another such fault line in American history. Sweeping changes in foreign policy occurred, largely in a direction now labeled (if vaguely defined) as "neo-conservativism." The course of history indeed might be different if President Bush and his closest advisors were not profoundly affected by the scholars and speakers populating the programs of organizations like the American Enterprise Institute and Hoover Institution.

Of course, we do not wish for future crises. But supporters of the freedom movement should remember that – in between those periods when public opinion is volatile – there is much work to be done, so that good ideas, based on the conservative principles of Ronald Reagan, will be the first off the shelf when history hands us our next surprise.

Personal Leadership

Before we get too far into this discussion of concrete ways to advance the freedom philosophy, let's talk about one very important lesson that gets right to heart of why Ronald Reagan was able to achieve so much.

It's about being a good person: meeting life's challenges with a resilient cheer and remembering all there is to be grateful for. Reagan's personality resonated humility, optimism and trustworthiness.

In her book, *When Character Was King*, Peggy Noonan wrote: "If you want to, you can bump into someone with a Reagan story just about anywhere you go. He has lived a long time, and he's led many lives. But what has surprised and even astonished me is that the stories are almost invariably about his graciousness, generosity, good humor...

I am still searching for an anecdote about Reagan that truly reflects badly on him. [Ideological opponents will] tell you Reagan was lazy, or naïve, or a bore. But they never say he was low or dishonest or untrustworthy. I think his character is the least criticized of any great political leader of the century."[70]

Maybe it seems like it would be easy to play the good sport, if you had a "charmed life" like Reagan with silver-screen fame, a storybook marriage, wealth and political power. But Reagan knew adversity: His family moved frequently when he was a boy as his alcoholic father lost job after job; he came of age during the Great Depression. And his first wife divorced him as his star-power in Hollywood faded. While he found a true soul mate in his second wife, Nancy, he had strained relations with his children.

Perhaps these ups and downs – and Reagan's understanding that all of lives are filled with them – explain why he connected so easily with such a large cross-section of the country. "I genuinely like people, and I think perhaps, people can tell," explained Reagan at the end of his presidency when asked for the secret to his popularity.[71]

Another lesson we take from Reagan is that greatness can spring from surprising places and unlikely experiences. John F. Kennedy's father famously groomed his sons for high office. But no one would have expected the zig-zags of Reagan's career to have produced a President – much less a great one. In retrospect, however, we see that Reagan gained

---

[70] Peggy Noonan, *When Character Was King* (New York: Viking Press, 2001), p. 82-83.

[71] Thomas Dye, *Who's Running America*, 5th edition (Englewood Cliffs, NJ: Prentice Hall, 1990), p. 71.

skills that were crucial to his future success at each stop along the way. His career in radio taught him to find the words to communicate his ideas, and his films and TV show made him comfortable under the public spotlight. Reagan's tough negotiating talents were honed as a labor leader in Hollywood. During that same period, he found himself in the whirlwind of the most intense communist infiltration the United States had yet seen, giving him an uncommon understanding of the threat. When Reagan's popularity as a film star waned, he found himself traveling the country as a corporate spokesman, meeting and talking with thousands of American citizens and mastering the stump speech. It's hard to imagine a job that would better simulate the experience of a political campaign.

Reagan turned these different life experiences to his advantage by approaching each of them as the quintessential happy warrior and team player, exhibiting honesty, humility and hard work.

Perhaps all this sounds simple. But, as Reagan used to say, there's a difference between *simple* and *easy*.

Reagan had the courage to walk away from the negotiating table in Reykjavik, where Gorbachev tried to get him to scrap his strategic defense initiative (SDI) in exchange for politically popular arms reductions. Reagan knew he would be beat up in the press for refusing this tempting offer. But Reagan did what he knew to be right – because he was in the habit of doing what was right.

Conservatives should take this to heart as much as any other of Reagan's lessons.

For our leaders to be trusted when it counts, they need to be trustworthy. For our ideas to be credible, we need to articulate them and hold them up to scrutiny, even among hostile audiences. While we all inevitably have flaws, we should strive to attain virtues. Honesty, compassion, and fairness take hold in society one person at a time.

There's a sizable part of the population that holds a negative view of conservatives, believing that we're greedy, mean-spirited, and actually wish misfortune upon people. Some will be unwilling to change those opinions, no matter what the evidence. But most with open eyes have open minds too. Being a good parent, spouse, friend, and neighbor – the kind of person that can be trusted to do what's right – is the first step to undoing negative stereotypes.

Educating and Inspiring the Next Generation

Trading our more cynical instincts for the happy warrior attitude of Ronald Reagan will also open opportunities to teach others. It has been said that people don't care what you know until they know that you care. If you have a reputation for honesty, compassion and fairness, you will discover that people will be more curious about your political opinions and will seek your advice in all areas of life.

This is important, especially with regard to the youngest generation of Americans. A future President of the United States is today running wild on a playground someplace in this country. Reagan conservatives should strive to educate him or her about what makes this country great.

As September 11 fades into memory, it becomes easier to return to the complacent attitudes of September 10. Our system of limited government and free enterprise has produced so much freedom, prosperity and tolerance that it is easy to take it all for granted. If we fail to do our duty by teaching the next generations to love their country and protect the freedoms at its core, the noble legacy and purpose of America could be forgotten and forever lost. The stakes are that high.

For this reason, it is important to take an interest in what children are learning – at school, from their peers, from the broader culture.

It's very troubling that so much of our popular culture gravitates to the lowest common denominator and glorifies moral relativism, instant gratification, and, at times, a dark nihilism that takes pleasure in others' pain. It may be impossible (or even unwise) to shield children entirely from ultra-violent video games, gross reality TV, or the degrading aspects of modern pop and rap music. But thoughtful parents should be protective of the innocence of their young children and use their moral authority to challenge cynical messages as they are encountered. Perhaps most important, you can be engaged in finding the positive alternatives that do exist out there. From the Harry Potter books to films like *Seabiscuit* that make history come alive, you have plenty of allies in shaping your children's interests in a positive direction.

Realize that, by clicking away from garbage TV shows and seeking out positive entertainment options, you are giving important feedback to Hollywood. Over recent years, socially conservative organizations have been documenting how family-oriented movies tend to be much more profitable than racy R-rated films. There has been a significant shift in production toward more G and PG movies as this fact has become part of Hollywood's conventional wisdom.

One of the great virtues of a market economy is that consumers can influence what gets produced through their purchasing decisions. In October 2003, we learned that CBS planned to broadcast a TV movie, *The Reagans*, which smeared Reagan's character and legacy with false stories. We created a Web site at *www.NoMoreCBS.com* to show the network it would be boycotted by thousands of Americans if they offered a biased account of Reagan's presidency. Almost overnight, we had 5,000 emails signing our petition and sending "God bless, Ronald Reagan" messages. It was very exciting to witness the spontaneous outpouring of emotion (and we only saw a fraction of it, as *www.BoycottCBS.com* appeared a day before ours and received many times the attention). Within a few days, CBS decided the movie should not be shown on broadcast television.

Some liberal critics said these petitions amounted to censorship, but they missed the point entirely. Free speech was the root of our petition. We acknowledged CBS was free to present its version of history, just as we are free to change our televisions to a different station – and to explain why we would make that choice. The uproar over CBS' *The Reagans* provides an encouraging lesson: Corporations can be influenced by a vocal grassroots coalition of private individuals.

Sadly, there are still more important areas of society where we can't "vote with our feet" and register dissatisfaction through individual choices. The way the American education system is constructed – with families unable to decide what school their kids are assigned to unless they can afford private school – it is difficult to influence change without lengthy battles with an entrenched bureaucracy.

Education reform is doubly important because, while Reagan worried that we were not teaching an "informed patriotism," some schools in America are actually teaching its opposite. Many school children know nothing about

Thomas Jefferson except that he was a slaveholder. While it is certainly appropriate to discuss the failings of history's great figures, the big picture is being lost. A well-publicized study by the Albert Shanker Institute from September 2003 found that public school textbooks are presenting a distorted view of the United States as an irredeemably flawed country.[72]

Parents need to ensure that young Americans understand the incredible accomplishments of George Washington and his generation. Namely, the creation of the world's first constitutional republic that combined democratic processes with protections of individual rights. By forming a government subservient to the people, and by restricting the government's authority so it would not grow tyrannical, the Founding Fathers created an opportunity for individual and societal advancement unlike anything in history.

True, the great men of that era failed to rid the country of the horrible institution of slavery.[73] Yet in this they were not unique: Cruelties like slavery have long, tragic histories on all continents. The remarkable legacy of George Washington, John Adams, Benjamin Franklin, Thomas Jefferson, and John Madison was in laying the foundation of a country that would become the world's brightest beacon of freedom.

---

[72] Associated Press, "Group Assails Schools on U.S. History: Story of U.S. Accomplishments Get Short Shrift in Nation's Schools, Report Says," September 9, 2003. See http://abcnews.go.com/wire/US/ap20030909_1425.html.

[73] Slavery, however, was condemned by all the leading founders and seven of the original 13 states outlawed slavery as an obvious extension of the logic of the country's founding Declaration that held "all men are created equal." See Thomas G. West, *Vindicating the Fathers: Race, Sex, Class and Justice in the Origins of America* (Lanham, MD: Rowman & Littlefield, 1997).

Distorted history is but one example of how America's students are ill-served by ideological prejudice. While there are a lot of great teachers out there, committed to learning and presenting an unbiased view of the facts, many believe their role is to proselytize for personal causes, while playing fast and loose with the facts when necessary.

For instance, one junior high school text book shows an illustration of the tips of New York City's skyscrapers barely emerging from floods, foreshadowed to be caused by global warming that could melt polar ice caps. It's an incredibly misleading visual, as even environmental pessimists predict that sea levels would rise no more than 6-40 inches under worst-case scenarios.[74]

Thankfully, there is a growing body of literature that challenges the hyperbole of the radical environmentalist movement and points out that doomsayers have been consistently wrong on the major issues of our times. They predicted that famine would impoverish the world by the end of the 20th Century, but the world's population is now better nourished than ever thanks to technological advances that give us more food from less land. Since the 1970s, alarmists in the environmental movement have flip-flopped on whether we headed toward catastrophic "global cooling" or catastrophic "global warming." Somehow they have not paused to consider whether our situation just might not be catastrophic, despite the fact that man's impact on global temperatures remains wrapped in uncertainty.

---

[74] Cited in Michael Sanera and Jane Shaw, *Facts Not Fear: Teaching Children About the Environment* (New York: Regnery Publishing Inc., 2nd edition, 1999).

It's important not to let our kids only see one side of the environmental debate. We need to point out that there is a tremendous human toll associated with policies promoted by groups like Greenpeace and the Sierra Club. For instance, after World War II, the pesticide DDT helped nearly eliminate the scourge of malaria, even in poor countries. Rachel Carson's famous 1962 book, *Silent Spring*, contended that DDT negatively effected bird reproduction. Though her allegations did not stand up to scientific scrutiny, DDT remains maligned and environmentalists fight against its use in developing countries, where it is the most cost-effective approach to stopping disease-spreading mosquitoes. Malaria is believed to cause up to 2.7 million deaths per year, mostly young children in Africa. Let these tragic numbers sound a cautionary warning to those who use junk science to "protect" poor nations from the advances brought by globalization.[75]

None of this is to discourage hearing opposing viewpoints on environmental policy or any other matter. But parents should be wary of how some members of today's education establishment use their authority to promote an anti-capitalist, environmentalist agenda at odds with the truth and traditional American values.

This bias and the more general failings of the government-run public school system have led many to seek K-12 alternatives for their own children, such as private schools and home schooling. And although a parent's first duty is to safeguard his or her own children, many are taking action to help other children, too. You may try to improve

---

[75] J. Gordon Edwards and Steven Milloy, "100 things you should know about DDT," available online at: http://www.junkscience.com/ddtfaq.htm.

the public school in your community by talking to the principal about teachers that spout political propaganda. Or help provide alternatives by supporting school choice programs that empower parents to move their children out of the bad schools and into more positive educational environments.

While still relatively young, the school choice movement is an inspiring example of how individuals can transform the policy debate. The idea of school choice was introduced in 1955 by the Nobel Prize-winning economist Milton Friedman. Changes in public policy have been slow in coming due to organized union opposition, but that has not stopped progress on many fronts. Philanthropists such as Pat Rooney, John Walton and John Kirtley have used their fortunes to pay for private scholarships – direct assistance so needy families can put their kids in better schools. The individuals who fund and run non-profit think tanks have pressed for incremental reforms that move us closer to the goal of educational freedom: The Pioneer Institute created a charter school movement in Massachusetts. Public interest law firms, like the Institute for Justice, have defended experiments with school vouchers and won court battles to affirm the constitutionality of programs in Milwaukee and Cleveland. Other individuals, such as Virginia Walden-Ford of D.C. Parents for School Choice have become grassroots advocates, mobilizing other local parents to get involved. Family by family, state by state, the school choice movement is gaining ground thanks to the dedication of private citizens who want better opportunities for all children.

Some day the school choice battle will be won and K-12 performance in the United States will rise to world-class standards. It's telling that our country already boasts world-beating colleges and universities, perhaps because there –

unlike in K-12 schooling – there is tremendous competition and students have virtually unlimited options.

Of course, American higher education is not perfect. For many, going to college is more a social experience than an academic exercise. It's a problem when college students squander educational opportunities, although it's one with a silver lining: So many universities are dominated by leftist faculty and administration members, skipping certain indoctrination sessions (also called "classes") might not be such a bad idea. This is especially true in many of pricey, prestige universities. We recommend that parents don't get distracted looking for the "best school" when they should look for the school most suited for their own child.

Parents who want to make sure that conservative ideas are given a fair hearing can send their children to schools like Grove City College, Hillsdale College, Patrick Henry College, or Claremont University. There are also educational summer seminars hosted by non-profit organizations, such as the Institute for Humane Studies' Summer Seminars or the Cato Institute's Summer University. Other organizations like The Heritage Foundation have excellent internship programs. The Leadership Institute has trained and placed thousands of young conservatives in positions in government, politics and the media. All these programs can expand college-age students' horizons and make them passionate about the power of ideas.

Supporting Sound Ideas for the Long Term

Conservatives tend to be personally generous, but they should be wary of unwittingly supporting left-wing ideas with their charitable giving. Many people give to their *alma mater* without a second's thought about how many professors have an agenda opposed to their own beliefs.

This is only a small part of a truly sad story in American life: the manner in which fortunes, built under the American system of free enterprise, are hijacked by people seeking to undermine that very system. When Henry Ford II resigned from the Ford Foundation, exasperated by its turn toward socialist causes, he left the country's then-biggest foundation without a member of the Ford family on its board of trustees. In his resignation letter, he wrote:

> *The foundation exists and thrives on the fruits of our economic system. The dividends of competitive enterprise make it all possible. A significant portion of the abundance created by U.S. business enables the foundation and like institutions to carry on their work. In effect, the foundation is a creature of capitalism — a statement that I'm sure would be shocking to many professional staff people in the field of philanthropy. It is hard to discern recognition of this in anything the foundation does. It is even more difficult to find an understanding of this in many of the institutions, particularly the universities, that are the beneficiaries of the foundation's grant programs.* [76]

Thankfully, there are organizations that cater to conservative philanthropists (large and small) and help protect donor intent. For instance, the Philanthropy Roundtable is an association of donors and foundation staff that assist donors in advancing freedom, opportunity and personal responsibility. Donors Trust actually administers charitable giving accounts for individuals who want to avoid the hassle of establishing an independent foundation, while

---

[76] Quoted in John J. Miller, *How Two Foundations Reshaped America* (Washington DC: Philanthropy Roundtable, 2003), p. 11.

making sure that their gifts remain focused on helping organizations that advance Reaganite principles.

Individuals who want to further the Reagan Revolution need to be thoughtful about the causes they support. Are you giving to organizations that lobby for more government involvement in problems that can be solved by civil society? Is your money being used to produce real changes, or is it recycled back into fundraising efforts? Is the school or research center that you fund advancing ideas at odds with the principles that make America great? If you answer "yes" to any of these, you ought to reconsider whether you could be more strategic in your giving, so that the Reagan vision has greater chance of being achieved.

One type of non-profit organization merits special consideration. Conservative and libertarian think tanks have been producing some of the most innovative work in the public policy arena. (Full disclosure: We have made careers working with such organizations.) Perhaps because academia is largely dominated by the Left, many who aspire to advance the ideas of Ronald Reagan and other advocates of limited government and free enterprise wind up working in think tanks.

A generation ago, few think tanks existed and most public policy debates involved politicians, bureaucrats, and interest groups with a stake in how the government spends money. Independent think tanks work to shape the long-term debate by injecting principles into politics.

While politicians must work within the band of what is "politically possible," think tanks develop and market ideas that can change what is considered feasible. Many of the ideas discussed in this book – from educational choice to medical savings accounts to social security privatization –

have been championed for decades by various market-oriented think tanks.

While Ronald Reagan deserves significant credit for his own promotion of conservative ideas, in several cases think tanks have provided the intellectual ammunition to change the debate. (Historians should further note the influence of the publications of the Foundation for Economic Education on Reagan himself.)

Reagan would no doubt be pleased by the continued development of the conservative think-tank movement over the past decade. In 1985, speaking to a group of conservatives at an event of the Conservative Political Action Committee, the President explained how an intellectual engine was driving the conservative movement to heights unimagined when Barry Goldwater was running for president:

> *In the past decade – all of a sudden, quietly, mysteriously – the Republican Party has become the party of ideas. We became the party of the most brilliant and dynamic young minds. I remember them, just a few years ago, running around scrawling Laffer curves on table napkins, going to symposia and talking about how social programs did not eradicate poverty, but entrenched it; writing studies on why the latest weird and unnatural idea from the social engineers is weird and unnatural. You were there. They were your ideas, your symposia, your books, and usually somebody else's table napkins.*[77]

A quintessential example is how Charles Murray's book, *Losing Ground*, published by the Manhattan Institute, changed the welfare debate. Before this book, critics of welfare were viewed as cold-hearted. Afterwards, it became

---

[77] Ronald Reagan, "Creators of the Future," March 8, 1985.

clear to people on both sides of the ideological divide that welfare as it then existed was harming poor people. By 1992, candidate Bill Clinton – certainly an adept reader of the political winds – was calling for "an end to welfare as we know it."

There is now a flourishing network of think tanks in the United States. Several organizations influence public policy at the national level in a variety of areas. The Heritage Foundation, the American Enterprise Institute and the Cato Institute are the largest, but there is also the National Center for Policy Analysis and the Competitive Enterprise Institute, among others. Some organizations are focused specifically on certain topics or audiences. The Galen Institute addresses health care issues. The Foundation for Individual Rights in Education is watchdog for academic freedom. Americans for Tax Reform gets politicians to pledge not to raise taxes. The Acton Institute creates programs to educate clergy about free-market ideas and the National Journalism Center provides aspiring members of the media with exposure to conservative perspectives. Another 40 organizations are classified as "state-based" think tanks, promoting conservative or libertarian ideas among state legislators.

Many of these organizations take inspiration from the story of the Institute of Economic Affairs, a small British think tank that doggedly built its reputation critiquing the economic policies of the Labor Party that dominated British politics for three decades after World War II. Margaret Thatcher credited the IEA with making possible her rise to Prime Minister and her success in enacting major market-oriented reforms that revitalized the British economy. "They were the few. They were right. And they saved Britain," Thatcher said of the institute's founding directors. "What we achieved could never have been done without the leadership of the IEA."[78]

There are also scores of think tanks advancing market-oriented ideas overseas. Some of the individuals working in these organizations are true heroes, laboring at grave personal risk to advance principled policies that threaten entrenched systems of privilege.

Hernando de Soto, a Peruvian economist who founded the Instituto Libertad y Demcoracia, saw his think tank's offices car-bombed in 1991. Nevertheless, De Soto has persevered and his recommendations about how developing nations can give the poor a stake in the market economy now command worldwide attention.

The long-term battle of ideas depends on building institutions to promote the ideas at the core of the Reagan vision. Today's think tanks are making important contributions – so much so that they have raised the ire of the Left who imagine themselves besieged by a "vast right-wing conspiracy."

Ironically, it is the Left that has vast resources at its command. The left-leaning Ford and MacArthur Foundations, just the two of them, combined to give $1 billion in grants in 2001, a figure that far exceeds the resources distributed to conservative non-profits.[79] Advancing the Reagan Revolution requires more dedication from conservatives to the task of building institutions educating the public about freedom.

---

[78] Gerald Frost, *Antony Fisher: Champion of Liberty* (London: Profile Books, 2002), p. 162.
[79] Using figures from publicly-available IRS Form 990 tax returns.

Supporting the intellectual conservative movement can be as simple as writing a check to support a non-profit institute, or exploring their Web sites and forwarding thoughtful articles to a friend. Visit the Atlas Economic Research Foundation's Web site, *www.atlasUSA.org,* for a comprehensive directory of market-oriented think tanks.

It's inspiring to think that an entire industry has developed thanks to the generosity of conservative donors (nearly all good think tanks refuse to take government funding). As a consequence, new minds are continually being engaged by independent researchers and advocates who cherish individual rights, free enterprise, and the rule of law under limited government.

Engaging the Media

Just as the Left is troubled by the effectiveness of think tanks in changing the intellectual debate, it also has become apoplectic about conservatives making inroads in the media. The popularity of conservative talk radio has shown that a large market exists for news and analysis that breaks from the eastern liberal status quo of Dan Rather, Tom Brokaw and Peter Jennings.

Similarly, Fox News has leapt ahead of its cable news rivals by distinguishing itself as a channel where conservative viewpoints get a fair hearing. Conservatives' thoughtful patronage of Fox News, and other individual programs, has sent a message to other news outlets. They no longer exclude conservatives to the extent that they did in the 1990s. Television viewers, tired of bias and the sensationalistic aspects of cable news, have also flocked to C-SPAN to receive unfiltered access to congressional hearings and for straightforward interviews of liberals and conservatives alike.

Of course, the rise of the Internet has forever changed how people obtain information and digest different viewpoints. Web logs (i.e., personal or group news and commentary Web sites), Web communities, and e-mail discussion groups have permanently broken the stranglehold on information that faced previous generations. Any one of us can become an independent reporter or news analyst with the click of a mouse.

All these are wonderful developments. But let's not become content. Many in the news and entertainment industries continue to view conservatives as curiosities, outside the bounds of respectable opinion. This is ironic. Journalism and the arts are full of passionate people who should be our allies in bringing opportunity to the poor, among the other benefits that come from a free society. Unfortunately, the vast majority of artists, actors, and musicians remain locked in a Marxist worldview that sees people in business as bad and people in government as good (except for those politicians who try to limit government!).

As a remedy, we need visionaries with bold plans to get conservative viewpoints into popular entertainment and to celebrate the ones that already exist. How long will it be before there's a pop culture magazine alternative to *Rolling Stone* and its ilk, the same way that Fox News provides an alternative to CNN? It's a shame that teens and young adults who want to read about their favorite bands or movie stars see those stories filtered through an anti-conservative, anti-capitalist lens.

Another avenue to pursue would be to develop documentaries or historical films on subjects dear to our hearts. It is fascinating to study the process by which "real history" becomes "accepted history." There is often a great disconnect. For instance, most people know little about the American West of the 19th Century except that it was the "Wild West" and was beset with bandits and gun violence. That's the impression one gets from a thousand TV westerns, but the facts are different. Despite the lack of strong law enforcement by government, frontier violence was much rarer than is urban violence today.[80]

The ruckus over CBS' *The Reagans* came about because conservatives sensed the film was a strategic move by the Hollywood Left to change how our 40th President is remembered. We need to get involved in filling the vacuum of historical entertainment so it not monopolized by those who want to caricature conservatives.

This isn't just an educational project. There are some great stories that ought to be told; reviving interest in history and celebrating inspiring heroes is just icing on the cake. Why haven't we seen movies about Harriet Tubman's Underground Railroad and the abolitionist career of William Lloyd Garrison? Or the Christian student resisters/martyrs in Nazi Germany that organized as The White Rose. Or the story of Poland's Solidarity labor movement that undermined Soviet Union's authority in Eastern Europe?

More historical programming – and more conservative programming – should become available as technology continues to cut the costs of media production. As prices fall, more multimedia entertainment will be available, via TV or

---

[80] Terry Anderson and P.J. Hill, "An American Experiment in Anarcho-Capitalism: The Not So Wild, Wild West," *Journal of Libertarian Studies*, Vol. 3, no. 1, 1979, p. 14.

the Internet, for niche audiences. Before long, we can expect the scholarship coming from conservative think tanks and intellectuals to be packaged into slick productions – just one example of the kind of innovative media that would advance the Reagan Revolution.

Making a Movement

Beyond the project of spreading our views and creating institutions to perpetuate this work, the conservative movement needs on-the-ground leadership in important policy battles and key elections – especially at the local levels.

This takes real energy and commitment. As advocates of limited government, we face the inevitable problem of needing to counter very passionate special interests who seek to gain advantages through government policies. As we discussed in Chapter 2, farm subsidies survive because their advocates are very motivated to keep receiving large amounts of taxpayers' money. Those harmed are far greater in number, but silent because the costs are spread broadly.

Conservative economist Steve Moore has built an effective political action committee, the Club for Growth, to represent individuals who want to support candidates friendly to growth-oriented, supply-side economic ideas. In 2002, 17 of the 19 political candidates backed by the club won. It is now the biggest source of funds for Republican candidates except for the Republican party itself (and, of course, Club for Growth only supports real conservatives who promise to advance Reaganite, growth-oriented economic policies).

Club for Growth is a great start. But we also need an "Army for Opportunity." We need individuals from all walks of life who are devoted to the Reaganite vision of individual rights, free enterprise and limited government – the formula for government that produces more opportunity and higher standards of living around the world. Once enlisted, these members could be "on call" to help achieve policy victories by spreading the message and mobilizing friends and relatives who share their aspirations.

Such a freedom movement would help offset the advantage that labor union support tends to give advocates of big government. For instance, voter referendums on school choice have failed because our opponents can call on the teachers' unions to supply the manpower for an anti-choice campaign. Our side has been much less successful in motivating volunteers to put in the hours to wave signs, make phone calls, and produce positive coverage in the media.

One can imagine that an active conservative membership could be built in many different ways. Potential organizational models are the American Association of Retired People and the 700 Club. Individuals could carry their freedom movement credit cards so that a percentage of their purchases go to charities promoting conservative ideas. The important thing is to give a large number of Americans a way to demonstrate their commitment to the principles that have made our country great. Many people are in the habit of giving to their church on a weekly basis, but their only contribution to the way our country is run are taxes (typically spent in ways they don't like) and irregular trips to the ballot box.

The bottom line is that we need more citizens like you to join the ranks of the Reagan Revolution. If you are willing and able to help, here's a quick "to-do list" of actions you can take – some of them you can do *today* – to begin advancing Ronald Reagan's vision.

Ten Things You Can Do
To Advance the Reagan Revolution

1. **Become Informed** – There are lots of fantastic places to get Reaganite perspectives on today's news. We catalog our favorites at www.ReaganVision.com. We suggest you:

   □ Visit our list of "reliable sources" on the Internet, and bookmark your favorites so you can visit often.

   □ Also, get informed on the think tanks and other freedom-oriented organizations in your area. (State Policy Network and the Atlas Economic Research Foundation have very good directories.) Attend events nearby, read reports, and see how you can contribute to their work.

2. **Spread the message** – What books or articles contributed to your enthusiasm for Reagan's ideas? Who are the people in your life that most influence the opinions of others? We recommend that you:

   □ Right now, make a list of the 10 close contacts of yours who would be great additions to the conservative movement.

   □ Order books to give them, so they get informed as well. (Of course, your authors think the book you're holding now is a great starting point for newcomers! But we also have catalogued other recommended titles on our www.ReaganVision.com Web site.)

3. **Vote with your Feet** – Or with the remote control of your TV, in order to send a message to today's producers of entertainment.

   □ Turn off *Fear Factor* now.

   □ Make an effort to discover how many options there are for folks who share your values. We've listed some movies at www.ReaganVision.com that celebrate individualism, free enterprise, and American pride. Let us know your favorites as well.

4. **Speak Your Mind** – Your opinion counts. Don't hesitate to express it.

   □ Is your local paper covering events with a liberal bias? Write the editor a letter tasking them to task. Or suggest they start publishing conservatives' syndicated columns on their op-ed page. Or, if the coverage is fair and balanced, give them a pat on the back for doing the right thing.

☐ Consider starting a Web log or "blog" of your own. It's remarkably easy to join the blogging revolution that allows anyone to self-publish. We have basic instructions on our site, or you can go direct to www.Blogspot.com and get started.

5. **Get Involved with Local Charities** - Before government began trying to solve every problem, the United States had a rich tradition of using private charity to meet the needs of the community. There are still many heroic "social entrepreneurs" working on the front lines.

☐ Get to know those people in your community that are doing good works, helping the less fortunate or aiding the families of those serving nobly in our military. Get involved and show them that you care.

☐ The school choice movement merits special mention here. As a society, we ought to aspire to putting a quality education within reach of all children. Unfortunately, many kids – especially poor ones in difficult situations – are stuck in underachieving schools. Private scholarship organizations like Arizona School Choice Trust saving children, one by one.

6. **Open Your Check Book** – Organizations promoting market-oriented ideas need your financial support. Virtually all of the country's largest foundations lean left. Moreover, most good free-market groups refuse to take government funding, something the left has no problem with.

☐ Research the organizations that are trying to make a difference in the world, and take one or more under your wing.

☐ If you are in position to make major gifts, make sure you are helping advance conservative/libertarian causes. Consider joining Philanthropy Roundtable (to be part of a network of donors with the same goals) or utilizing Donors Trust (providing philanthropic services for donors dedicated to advancing the ideal of freedom).

7. **Close Your Check Book** – If opening your check book to new charities seems easier said than done, you may be able to do some good by *closing* your check book as well.

☐ Does your alma mater truly make a positive contribution? If you're concerned that your donations are funding leftists, you should see if you can restrict your donations to make sure it goes to the ideas you support.

☐ Scrutinize other affiliations you have. Do they support ideas that are hostile to your core principles? If so, think about whether you can drive reform from within, or perhaps it's not worth remaining involved with such a group.

8. **Question candidates** - Don't blindly follow any party. Before signing on to help a candidate, see what you can learn about him or her from Club for Growth or Americans for Tax Reform. These are groups that care about making sure conservatives are elected – not just Republicans.

☐ Go to candidates' events and ask where they stand on critical issues. You'll not only be educating yourself about their positions, but you'll enlighten the audience and the candidates about your concerns and your commitment to Reagan's vision.

☐ Support candidates that support the cause. Help out with campaign events, walk precincts, lick envelopes for candidates that will be faithful to good principles.

9. **Consider running for office** – The Reaganite team needs a deeper bench, so consider running for local office.

☐ You can positively affect your community by taking part in local meetings, or by getting elected to your school board or city council.

☐ Use your position in local government to inform your other policy makers about work your doing at the local level, and about the principles that drive your interest in public service.

10. **Dream Big** – There's great power in setting your sights high. Reagan had a knack for transforming the public policy agenda -- for instance, in pursuing SDI to make nuclear weapons obsolete, rather than merely holding ground to contain Soviet imperialism. We need to work on the big picture as well, so we do not get lost in fighting for small victories.

☐ Write down how you would like to see the world ten years from now. Picture it in your mind. Think about what changes would have to happen. Hold onto that description, so you can look back on it in later years.

☐ As a final step, share those thoughts of yours with us at www.ReaganVision.com. And then roll up your sleeves and get ready to work to achieve the Reagan Revolution.

If we are successful in popularizing a freedom movement and mobilizing a large number of dedicated citizens, our prospects for success will expand dramatically. We will be better able to hold elected representatives to account.

The Long Battle Ahead

The last paragraphs of Ronald Reagan's farewell letter to the American people of 1994, when he announced his affliction with Alzheimer's disease, read:

> *In closing, let me thank you, the American people, for giving me the great honor of allowing me to serve as your president. When the Lord calls me home, whenever that may be, I will leave the greatest love for this country of ours and eternal optimism for its future.*
>
> *I now begin the journey that will lead me into the sunset of my life. I know that for America there will always be a bright dawn ahead.*

We all can share in Reagan's optimism. The principles of freedom put us on the right side of history. We can feel confident that our side will ultimately prevail. True, there will never be a final victory as we need eternal vigilance to safeguard liberty. But we should recognize that we are on the cusp of big advances.

Look at our enormous progress so far. In the early decades of the 20th Century, socialism was on the march. Individuals like Albert Jay Nock, who we now view as forerunners of the modern conservative movement, viewed their role as that of a "remnant" – with no hope of convincing the general public, but dedicated to preserving ideas for future generations like monks in the Dark Ages.[81] Yet thanks

---

[81] George Nash, *The Conservative Intellectual Movement in America since 1945* (Wilmington, DC: Intercollegiate Studies Institute, 1996), p.11.

to a dedicated cadre of scholars, philanthropists and entrepreneurs, the intellectual tide has turned in a big way. As we have documented in this book, Reagan himself deserves great credit for fusing the different strains of conservative thought and giving the philosophy an optimistic energy that it previously lacked.

Conservativism is on its way to becoming a majority movement. This is the time to translate ideological victory into electoral successes and policy accomplishments. In 2004 and beyond, Republicans can win and have it mean something for completing the Reagan Revolution.

Our Rendezvous with Destiny

Achieving the next victories of the conservative movement depends on each of us, the American citizens that Ronald Reagan believed in with such confidence. As you close this book, we hope to leave you with one question: Will you do your part to advance Reagan's vision?

During the 1976 Republican National Convention, Reagan offered stirring remarks about a letter he had been asked to write for a time capsule to be opened 100 years later on the country's tri-centennial. "Let your own mind turn to that task," he challenged the audience. Reagan explained how he wanted to write about the domestic problems facing the country, and the tense situation in the Cold War in which "the great powers have poised and aimed at each other horrible missiles of destruction, nuclear weapons that can in a matter of minutes arrive at each other's country and destroy, virtually, the civilized world we live in."

Reagan continued:

And suddenly it dawned on me, those who would read this letter a hundred years from now will know whether those missiles were fired. They will know whether we met our challenge. Whether they have the freedoms that we have known up until now will depend on what we do here.[82]

Thankfully we do know most of the answers to the questions Reagan considered that summer night, and history will note that Reagan indeed met his "rendezvous with destiny" with courage and success. But those of us still engaged in the important challenges of our time must take to heart the urgency with which Reagan spoke.

In our daily lives, each of us in some way has the opportunity to advance the Reagan Revolution. From the campus activist to powerful politicians to concerned parents and grandparents hoping to guide a new generation to a better future, each of us can help in achieving Reagan's vision.

As Reagan would have reminded us, it's a battle worth fighting and worth winning:

Once during the campaign, I said, 'This is a wonderful time to be alive,' and I meant that. I meant that we're lucky not to live in pale and timid times. We've been blessed with the opportunity to stand for something – for liberty and freedom and fairness. And these are things worth fighting for, worth devoting our lives to. And we have good reason to be hopeful and optimistic. We've made much progress already. So, let us go forth with good cheer and stout hearts – happy warriors out to seize back a country and a world to freedom.[83]

---

[82] Ronald Reagan, "Remarks at the Republican National Convention," August 19, 1976. Available at: http://www.thereaganlegacy.com/version2/speechesdetails.asp?sID=20.

[83] Ronald Reagan, "Creators of the Future," March 8, 1985.

Appendix

Selected Reagan Speeches

A Time for Choosing

The address that launched Ronald Reagan's political career was broadcast on national television on October 27, 1964. Reagan spoke on behalf of Barry Goldwater's campaign for the presidency.

Thank you very much. Thank you and good evening. The sponsor has been identified, but unlike most television programs, the performer hasn't been provided with a script. As a matter of fact, I have been permitted to choose my own ideas regarding the choice that we face in the next few weeks.

I have spent most of my life as a Democrat. I recently have seen fit to follow another course. I believe that the issues confronting us cross party lines. Now, one side in this campaign has been telling us that the issues of this election are the maintenance of peace and prosperity. The line has been used "We've never had it so good."

But I have an uncomfortable feeling that this prosperity isn't something on which we can base our hopes for the future. No nation in history has ever survived a tax burden that reached a third of its national income. Today, 37 cents of every dollar earned in this country is the tax collector's share, and yet our government continues to spend $17 million a day more than the government takes in. We haven't balanced our budget 28 out of the last 34 years. We have raised our debt limit three times in the last twelve months, and now our national debt is one and a half times bigger than all the combined debts of all the nations in the world. We have $15 billion in gold in our treasury—we don't own an ounce. Foreign dollar claims are $27.3 billion, and we have just had announced that the dollar of 1939 will now purchase 45 cents in its total value.

As for the peace that we would preserve, I wonder who among us would like to approach the wife or mother whose husband or son has died in South Vietnam and ask them if they think this is a peace that should be maintained indefinitely. Do they mean peace, or do they mean we just want to be left in peace? There can be no real peace while one American is dying some place in the world for the rest of us. We are at war with the most dangerous enemy that has ever faced mankind in his long climb from the swamp to the stars, and it has been said if we lose that war, and in doing so lose this way of freedom of ours, history will record with the greatest astonishment that those who had the most to lose did the least to prevent its happening. Well, I think it's time we ask ourselves if we still know the freedoms that were intended for us by the Founding Fathers.

Not too long ago two friends of mine were talking to a Cuban refugee, a businessman who had escaped from Castro, and in the midst of his story one of my friends turned to the other and said, "We don't know how lucky we are." And the Cuban stopped and said, "How lucky you are? *I had someplace to escape to.*" In that sentence he told us the entire story. If we lose freedom here, there is no place to escape to. This is the last stand on Earth. And this idea that government is beholden to the people, that it has no other source of power except the sovereign people, is still the newest and most unique idea in all the long history of man's relation to man. This is the issue of this election. Whether we believe in our capacity for self-government or whether we abandon the American revolution and confess that a little intellectual elite in a far-distant capital can plan our lives for us better than we can plan them ourselves.

You and I are told increasingly that we have to choose between a left or right, but I would like to suggest that there is no such thing as a left or right. There is only an up or down—up to a man's age-old dream, the ultimate in individual freedom consistent with law and order—or down to the ant heap of totalitarianism, and regardless of their sincerity, their humanitarian motives, those who would trade our freedom for security have embarked on this downward course.

In this vote-harvesting time, they use terms like the "Great Society," or as we were told a few days ago by the President, we must accept a "greater government activity in the affairs of the people." But they have been a little more explicit in the past and among themselves—and all of the things that I now will quote have appeared in print. These are not Republican accusations. For example, they have voices that say "the cold war will end through acceptance of a not undemocratic socialism." Another voice says that the profit motive has become outmoded, it must be replaced by the incentives of the welfare state; or our traditional system of individual freedom is incapable of solving the complex problems of the 20th century. Senator Fullbright has said at Stanford University that the Constitution is outmoded. He referred to the president as our moral teacher and our leader, and he said he is hobbled in his task by the restrictions in power imposed on him by this antiquated document. He must be freed so that he can do for us what he knows is best. And Senator Clark of Pennsylvania, another articulate spokesman, defines liberalism as "meeting the material needs of the masses through the full power of centralized government." Well, I for one resent it when a representative of the people refers to you and me—the free man and woman of this country—as "the masses." This is a term we haven't applied to ourselves in America. But beyond that, "the full power of centralized government"—this was the very thing the Founding

Fathers sought to minimize. They knew that governments don't control things. A government can't control the economy without controlling people. And they know when a government sets out to do that, it must use force and coercion to achieve its purpose. They also knew, those Founding Fathers, that outside of its legitimate functions, government does nothing as well or as economically as the private sector of the economy.

Now, we have no better example of this than the government's involvement in the farm economy over the last 30 years. Since 1955, the cost of this program has nearly doubled. One-fourth of farming in America is responsible for 85% of the farm surplus. Three-fourths of farming is out on the free market and has known a 21% increase in the per capita consumption of all its produce. You see, that one-fourth of farming is regulated and controlled by the federal government. In the last three years we have spent $43 in feed grain program for every bushel of corn we don't grow.

Senator Humphrey last week charged that Barry Goldwater as President would seek to eliminate farmers. He should do his homework a little better, because he will find out that we have had a decline of 5 million in the farm population under these government programs. He will also find that the Democratic administration has sought to get from Congress an extension of the farm program to include that three-fourths that is now free. He will find that they have also asked for the right to imprison farmers who wouldn't keep books as prescribed by the federal government. The Secretary of Agriculture asked for the right to seize farms through condemnation and resell them to other individuals. And contained in that same program was a provision that would have allowed the federal government to remove 2 million farmers from the soil.

At the same time, there has been an increase in the Department of Agriculture employees. There is now one for every 30 farms in the United States, and still they can't tell us how 66 shiploads of grain headed for Austria disappeared without a trace and Billie Sol Estes never left shore.

Every responsible farmer and farm organization has repeatedly asked the government to free the farm economy, but who are farmers to know what is best for them? The wheat farmers voted against a wheat program. The government passed it anyway. Now the price of bread goes up; the price of wheat to the farmer goes down.

Meanwhile, back in the city, under urban renewal the assault on freedom carries on. Private property rights are so diluted that public interest is almost anything that a few government planners decide it should be. In a program that takes for the needy and gives to the greedy, we see such spectacles as in Cleveland, Ohio, a million-and-a-half-dollar building completed only three years ago must be destroyed to make way for what government officials call a "more compatible use of the land." The President tells us he is now going to start building public housing units in the thousands where heretofore we have only built them in the hundreds. But FHA and the Veterans Administration tell us that they have 120,000 housing units they've taken back through mortgage foreclosures. For three decades, we have sought to solve the problems of unemployment through government planning, and the more the plans fail, the more the planners plan. The latest is the Area Redevelopment Agency. They have just declared Rice County, Kansas, a depressed area. Rice County, Kansas, has two hundred oil wells, and the 14,000 people there have over $30 million on deposit in personal savings in their banks. When the government tells you you're depressed, lie down and be depressed.

We have so many people who can't see a fat man standing beside a thin one without coming to the conclusion that the fat man got that way by taking advantage of the thin one. So they are going to solve all the problems of human misery through government and government planning. Well, now, if government planning and welfare had the answer and they've had almost 30 years of it, shouldn't we expect government to almost read the score to us once in a while? Shouldn't they be telling us about the decline each year in the number of people needing help? The reduction in the need for public housing?

But the reverse is true. Each year the need grows greater, the program grows greater. We were told four years ago that 17 million people went to bed hungry each night. Well, that was probably true. They were all on a diet. But now we are told that 9.3 million families in this country are poverty-stricken on the basis of earning less than $3,000 a year. Welfare spending is 10 times greater than in the dark depths of the Depression. We are spending $45 billion on welfare. Now do a little arithmetic, and you will find that if we divided the $45 billion up equally among those 9 million poor families, we would be able to give each family $4,600 a year, and this added to their present income should eliminate poverty! Direct aid to the poor, however, is running only about $600 per family. It would seem that someplace there must be some overhead.

So now we declare "war on poverty," or "you, too, can be a Bobby Baker!" Now, do they honestly expect us to believe that if we add $1 billion to the $45 million we are spending...one more program to the 30-odd we have—and remember, this new program doesn't replace any, it just duplicates existing programs—do they believe that poverty is suddenly going to disappear by magic? Well, in all fairness I should explain that there is one part of the new program that isn't duplicated. This is the youth feature. We are now going to solve the dropout problem, juvenile delinquency, by reinstituting something like the old CCC camps, and we are going to put our young people in camps, but again we do some arithmetic, and we find that we are going to spend each year just on room and board for each young person that we help $4,700 a year! We can send them to Harvard for $2,700! Don't get me wrong. I'm not suggesting that Harvard is the answer to juvenile delinquency.

But seriously, what are we doing to those we seek to help? Not too long ago, a judge called me here in Los Angeles. He told me of a young woman who had come before him for a divorce. She had six children, was pregnant with her seventh. Under his questioning, she revealed her husband was a laborer earning $250 a month. She wanted a divorce so that she could get an $80 raise. She is eligible for $330 a month in the Aid to Dependent Children Program. She got the idea from two women in her neighborhood who had already done that very thing.

Yet anytime you and I question the schemes of the do-gooders, we are denounced as being against their humanitarian goals. They say we are always "against" things, never "for" anything. Well, the trouble with our liberal friends is not that they are ignorant, but that they know so much that isn't so. We are for a provision that destitution should not follow unemployment by reason of old age, and to that end we have accepted Social Security as a step toward meeting the problem.

But we are against those entrusted with this program when they practice deception regarding its fiscal shortcomings, when they charge that any criticism of the program means that we want to end payments to those who depend on them for livelihood. They have called it insurance to us in a hundred million pieces of literature. But then they appeared before the Supreme Court and they testified that it was a welfare program. They only use the term "insurance" to sell it to the people. And they said Social Security dues are a tax for the general use of the government, and the government has used that tax. There is no fund, because Robert Byers, the actuarial head, appeared before a congressional committee and admitted that Social Security as of this moment is $298 billion in the hole. But he said there should be no cause for worry because as long as they have the power to tax, they could always take away from the people whatever they needed to bail them out of trouble! And they are doing just that.

A young man, 21 years of age, working at an average salary...his Social Security contribution would, in the open market, buy him an insurance policy that would guarantee $220 a month at age 65. The government promises $127. He could live it up until he is 31 and then take out a policy that would pay more than Social Security. Now, are we so lacking in business sense that we can't put this program on a sound basis so that people who do require those payments will find that they can get them when they are due...that the cupboard isn't bare? Barry Goldwater thinks we can.

At the same time, can't we introduce voluntary features that would permit a citizen who can do better on his own to be excused upon presentation of evidence that he had made provisions for the non-earning years? Shouldn't we allow a widow with children to work, and not lose the benefits supposedly paid for by her deceased husband? Shouldn't you and I be allowed to declare who our beneficiaries will be under these programs, which we cannot do? I think we are for telling our senior citizens that no one in this country should be denied medical care because of a lack of funds. But I think we are against forcing all citizens, regardless of need, into a compulsory government program, especially when we have such examples, as announced last week, when France admitted that their Medicare program was now bankrupt. They've come to the end of the road.

In addition, was Barry Goldwater so irresponsible when he suggested that our government give up its program of deliberate planned inflation so that when you do get your Social Security pension, a dollar will buy a dollar's worth, and not 45 cents' worth?

I think we are for an international organization, where the nations of the world can seek peace. But I think we are against subordinating American interests to an organization that has become so structurally unsound that today you can muster a two-thirds vote on the floor of the General Assembly among the nations that represent less than 10 percent of the world's population. I think we are against the hypocrisy of assailing our allies because here and there they cling to a colony, while we engage in a conspiracy of silence and never open our mouths about the millions of people enslaved in Soviet colonies in the satellite nations.

I think we are for aiding our allies by sharing of our material blessings with those nations which share in our fundamental beliefs, but we are against doling out money government to government, creating bureaucracy, if not socialism, all over the world. We set out to help 19 countries. We are helping 107. We spent $146 billion. With that money, we bought a $2 million yacht for Haile Selassie. We bought dress suits for Greek undertakers, extra wives for Kenyan government officials. We bought a thousand TV sets for a place where they have no electricity. In the last six years, 52 nations have bought $7 billion worth of our gold, and all 52 are receiving foreign aid from this country.

No government ever voluntarily reduces itself in size. Government programs, once launched, never disappear. Actually, a government bureau is the nearest thing to eternal life we'll ever see on this Earth. Federal employees number 2.5 million, and federal, state, and local, one out of six of the nation's work force is employed by the government. These proliferating bureaus with their thousands of regulations have cost us many of our constitutional safeguards. How many of us realize that today federal agents can invade a man's property without a warrant? They can impose a fine without a formal hearing. let alone a trial by jury, and they can seize and sell his property in auction to enforce the payment of that fine. In Chico County, Arkansas, James Wier over planted his rice allotment. The government obtained a $17,000 judgment, and a U.S. marshal sold his 950-acre farm at auction. The government said it was necessary as a warning to others to make the system work. Last February 19 at the University of Minnesota, Norman Thomas, six-time candidate for President on the Socialist Party ticket, said, "If Barry Goldwater became President, he would stop the advance of socialism in the United States." I think that's exactly what he will do.

As a former Democrat, I can tell you Norman Thomas isn't the only man who has drawn this parallel to socialism with the present administration. Back in 1936, Mr. Democrat himself, Al Smith, the great American, came before the American people and charged that the leadership of his party was taking the party of Jefferson, Jackson, and Cleveland down the road under the banners of Marx, Lenin, and Stalin. And he walked away from his party, and he never returned to the day he died, because to this day, the leadership of that party has been taking that party, that honorable party, down the road in the image of the labor socialist party of England. Now it doesn't require expropriation or confiscation of private property or business to impose socialism on a people. What does it mean whether you hold the deed or the title to your business or property if the government holds the power of life and death over that business or property? Such machinery already exists. The government can find some charge to bring against any concern it chooses to prosecute. Every businessman has his own tale of harassment. Somewhere a perversion has taken place. Our natural, inalienable rights are now considered to be a dispensation of government, and freedom has never been so fragile, so close to slipping from our grasp as it is at this moment. Our Democratic opponents seem unwilling to debate these issues. They want to make you and I believe that this is a contest between two men...that we are to choose just between two personalities.

Well, what of this man that they would destroy? And in destroying, they would destroy that which he represents, the ideas that you and I hold dear. Is he the brash and shallow and trigger-happy man they say he is? Well, I have been privileged to know him "when." I knew him long before he ever dreamed of trying for high office, and I can tell you personally I have never known a man in my life I believe so incapable of doing a dishonest or dishonorable thing.

This is a man who in his own business, before he entered politics, instituted a profit-sharing plan, before unions had ever thought of it. He put in health and medical insurance for all his employees. He took 50 percent of the profits before taxes and set up a retirement program, a pension plan for all his employees. He sent checks for life to an employee who was ill and couldn't work. He provided nursing care for the children of mothers who work in the stores. When Mexico was ravaged by floods from the Rio Grande, he climbed in his airplane and flew medicine and supplies down there.

An ex-GI told me how he met him. It was the week before Christmas during the Korean War, and he was at the Los Angeles airport trying to get a ride home to Arizona for Christmas, and he said that there were a lot of servicemen there and no seats available on the planes. Then a voice came over the loudspeaker and said, "Any men in uniform wanting a ride to Arizona, go to runway such-and-such," and they went down there, and there was this fellow named Barry Goldwater sitting in his plane. Every day in the weeks before Christmas, all day long, he would load up the plane, fly to Arizona, fly them to their homes, then fly back over to get another load.

During the hectic split-second timing of a campaign, this is a man who took time out to sit beside an old friend who was dying of cancer. His campaign managers were understandably impatient, but he said, "There aren't many left who care what happens to her. I'd like her to know I care." This is a man who said to his 19-year-old son, "There is no foundation like the rock of honesty and fairness, and when you begin to build your life upon that rock, with the cement of the faith in God that you have, then you have a real start." This is not a man who could carelessly send other people's sons to war. And that is the issue of this campaign that makes all of the other problems I have discussed academic, unless we realize that we are in a war that must be won.

Those who would trade our freedom for the soup kitchen of the welfare state have told us that they have a utopian solution of peace without victory. They call their policy "accommodation." And they say if we only avoid any direct confrontation with the enemy, he will forget his evil ways and learn to love us. All who oppose them are indicted as warmongers. They say we offer simple answers to complex problems. Well, perhaps there is a simple answer—not an easy answer—but simple.

If you and I have the courage to tell our elected officials that we want our national policy based upon what we know in our hearts is morally right. We cannot buy our security, our freedom from the threat of the bomb by committing an immorality so great as saying to a billion now in slavery behind the Iron Curtain, "Give up your dreams of freedom because to save our own skin, we are willing to make a deal with your slave masters." Alexander Hamilton said, "A nation which can prefer disgrace to danger is prepared for a master, and deserves one." Let's set the record straight. There is no argument over the choice between peace and war, but there is only one guaranteed way you can have peace—and you can have it in the next second—surrender.

Admittedly there is a risk in any course we follow other than this, but every lesson in history tells us that the greater risk lies in appeasement, and this is the specter our well-meaning liberal friends refuse to face—that their policy of accommodation is appeasement, and it gives no choice between peace and war, only between fight and surrender. If we continue to accommodate, continue to back and retreat, eventually we have to face the final demand—the ultimatum. And what then? When Nikita Khrushchev has told his people he knows what our answer will be? He has told them that we are retreating under the pressure of the Cold War, and someday when the time comes to deliver the ultimatum, our surrender will be voluntary because by that time we will have weakened from within spiritually, morally, and economically. He believes this because from our side he has heard voices pleading for "peace at any price" or "better Red than dead," or as one commentator put it, he would rather "live on his knees than die on his feet." And therein lies the road to war, because those voices don't speak for the rest of us. You and I know and do not believe that life is so dear and peace so sweet as to be purchased at the price of chains and slavery. If nothing in life is worth dying for, when did this begin—just in the face of this enemy? Or should Moses have told the children of Israel to live in slavery under the pharaohs? Should Christ have refused the cross? Should the patriots at Concord Bridge have thrown down their guns and refused to fire the shot heard 'round the world? The martyrs of history were not fools, and our honored dead who gave their lives to stop the advance of the Nazis didn't die in vain. Where, then, is the road to peace? Well, it's a simple answer after all.

You and I have the courage to say to our enemies, "There is a price we will not pay. There is a point beyond which they must not advance." This is the meaning in the phrase of Barry Goldwater's "peace through strength." Winston Churchill said that "the destiny of man is not measured by material computation. When great forces are on the move in the world, we learn we are spirits—not animals." And he said, "There is something going on in time and space, and beyond time and space, which, whether we like it or not, spells duty."

You and I have a rendezvous with destiny. We will preserve for our children this, the last best hope of man on Earth, or we will sentence them to take the last step into a thousand years of darkness.

We will keep in mind and remember that Barry Goldwater has faith in us. He has faith that you and I have the ability and the dignity and the right to make our own decisions and determine our own destiny.

Thank you very much.

First Inaugural Address

On January 20, 1981, Ronald Reagan was sworn into office as the 40[h] President of the United States of America. His inaugural address was given on the western front of the U.S. Capitol.

Senator Hatfield, Mr. Chief Justice, Mr. President, Vice President Bush, Vice President Mondale, Senator Baker, Speaker O'Neill, Reverend Moomaw, and my fellow citizens.

To a few of us here today this is a solemn and most momentous occasion, and yet in the history of our nation it is a commonplace occurrence. The orderly transfer of authority as called for in the Constitution routinely takes place, as it has for almost two centuries, and few of us stop to think how unique we really are. In the eyes of many in the world, this every-four-year ceremony we accept as normal is nothing less than a miracle.

Mr. President, I want our fellow citizens to know how much you did to carry on this tradition. By your gracious cooperation in the transition process, you have shown a watching world that we are a united people pledged to maintaining a political system which guarantees individual liberty to a greater degree than any other, and I thank you and your people for all your help in maintaining the continuity which is the bulwark of our republic. The business of our nation goes forward. These United States are confronted with an economic affliction of great proportions. We suffer from the longest and one of the worst sustained inflations in our national history. It distorts our economic decisions, penalizes thrift, and crushes the struggling young and the fixed-income elderly alike. It threatens to shatter the lives of millions of our people.

Idle industries have cast workers into unemployment, human misery, and personal indignity. Those who do work are denied a fair return for their labor by a tax system which penalizes successful achievement and keeps us from maintaining full productivity.

But great as our tax burden is, it has not kept pace with public spending. For decades we have piled deficit upon deficit, mortgaging our future and our children's future for the temporary convenience of the present. To continue this long trend is to guarantee tremendous social, cultural, political, and economic upheavals.

You and I, as individuals, can, by borrowing, live beyond our means, but for only a limited period of time. Why, then, should we think that collectively, as a nation, we're not bound by that same limitation? We must act today in order to preserve tomorrow. And let there be no misunderstanding: We are going to begin to act, beginning today.

The economic ills we suffer have come upon us over several decades. They will not go away in days, weeks, or months, but they will go away. They will go away because we as Americans have the capacity now, as we've had in the past, to do whatever needs to be done to preserve this last and greatest bastion of freedom.

In this present crisis, government is not the solution to our problem; government is the problem. From time to time we've been tempted to believe that society has become too complex to be managed by self-rule, that government by an elite group is superior to government for, by, and of the people. Well, if no one among us is capable of governing himself, then who among us has the capacity to govern someone else? All of us together, in and out of government, must bear the burden. The solutions we seek must be equitable, with no one group singled out to pay a higher price.

We hear much of special interest groups. Well, our concern must be for a special interest group that has been too long neglected. It knows no sectional boundaries or ethnic and racial divisions, and it crosses political party lines. It is made up of men and women who raise our food, patrol our streets, man our mines and factories, teach our children, keep our homes, and heal us when we're sick—professionals, industrialists, shopkeepers, clerks, cabbies, and truck drivers. They are, in short, "we the people," this breed called Americans.

Well, this administration's objective will be a healthy, vigorous, growing economy that provides equal opportunities for all Americans, with no barriers born of bigotry or discrimination. Putting America back to work means putting all Americans back to work. Ending inflation means freeing all Americans from the terror of runaway living costs. All must share in the productive work of this "new beginning," and all must share in the bounty of a revived economy. With the idealism and fair play which are the core of our system and our strength, we can have a strong and prosperous America, at peace with itself and the world.

So, as we begin, let us take inventory. We are a nation that has a government—not the other way around. And this makes us special among the nations of the Earth. Our government has no power except that granted it by the people. It is time to check and reverse the growth of government, which shows signs of having grown beyond the consent of the governed.

It is my intention to curb the size and influence of the federal establishment and to demand recognition of the distinction between the powers granted to the federal government and those reserved to the states or to the people. All of us need to be reminded that the federal government did not create the states; the states created the federal government.

Now, so there will be no misunderstanding, it's not my intention to do away with government. It is rather to make it work—work with us, not over us; to stand by our side, not ride on our back. Government can and must provide opportunity, not smother it; foster productivity, not stifle it.

If we look to the answer as to why for so many years we achieved so much, prospered as no other people on earth, it was because here in this land we unleashed the energy and individual genius of man to a greater extent than has ever been done before. Freedom and the dignity of the individual have been more available and assured here than in any other place on earth. The price for this freedom at times has been high, but we have never been unwilling to pay the price.

It is no coincidence that our present troubles parallel and are proportionate to the intervention and intrusion in our lives that result from unnecessary and excessive growth of government. It is time for us to realize that we're too great a nation to limit ourselves to small dreams. We're not, as some would have us believe, doomed to an inevitable decline. I do not believe in a fate that will fall on us no matter what we do. I do believe in a fate that will fall on us if we do nothing. So, with all the creative energy at our command, let us begin an era of national renewal. Let us renew our determination, our courage, and our strength. And let us renew our faith and our hope.

We have every right to dream heroic dreams. Those who say that we're in a time when there are no heroes, they just don't know where to look. You can see heroes every day going in and out of factory gates. Others, a handful in number, produce enough food to feed all of us and then the world beyond. You meet heroes across a counter, and they're on both sides of that counter. There are entrepreneurs with faith in themselves and faith in an idea who create new jobs, new wealth and opportunity. They're individuals and families whose taxes support the government and whose voluntary gifts support church, charity, culture, art, and education. Their patriotism is quiet, but deep. Their values sustain our national life.

Now, I have used the words "they" and "their" in speaking of these heroes. I could say "you" and "your," because I'm addressing the heroes of whom I speak—you, the citizens of this blessed land. Your dreams, your hopes, your goals are going to be the dreams, the hopes, and the goals of this administration, so help me God.

We shall reflect the compassion that is so much a part of your makeup. How can we love our country and not love our countrymen; and loving them, reach out a hand when they fall, heal them when they're sick, and provide opportunity to make them self-sufficient so they will be equal in fact and not just in theory?

Can we solve the problems confronting us? Well, the answer is an unequivocal and emphatic "yes." To paraphrase Winston Churchill, I did not take the oath I've just taken with the intention of presiding over the dissolution of the world's strongest economy.

In the days ahead I will propose removing the roadblocks that have slowed our economy and reduced productivity. Steps will be taken aimed at restoring the balance between the various levels of government. Progress may be slow, measured in inches and feet, not miles, but we will progress. It is time to reawaken this industrial giant, to get government back within its means, and to lighten our punitive tax burden. And these will be our first priorities, and on these principles there will be no compromise.

On the eve of our struggle for independence a man who might have been one of the greatest among the Founding Fathers, Dr. Joseph Warren, president of the Massachusetts Congress, said to his fellow Americans, "Our country is in danger, but not to be despaired of . . . On you depend the fortunes of America. You are to decide the important questions upon which rests the happiness and the liberty of millions yet unborn. Act worthy of yourselves." Well, I believe we, the Americans of today, are ready to act worthy of ourselves, ready to do what must be done to ensure happiness and liberty for ourselves, our children, and our children's children. And as we renew ourselves here in our own land, we will be seen as having greater strength throughout the world. We will again be the exemplar of freedom and a beacon of hope for those who do not now have freedom.

To those neighbors and allies who share our freedom, we will strengthen our historic ties and assure them of our support and firm commitment. We will match loyalty with loyalty. We will strive for mutually beneficial relations. We will not use our friendship to impose on their sovereignty, for our own sovereignty is not for sale. As for the enemies of freedom, those who are potential adversaries, they will be reminded that peace is the highest aspiration of the American people. We will negotiate for it, sacrifice for it; we will not surrender for it, now or ever.

Our forbearance should never be misunderstood. Our reluctance for conflict should not be misjudged as a failure of will. When action is required to preserve our national security, we will act. We will maintain sufficient strength to prevail if need be, knowing that if we do so we have the best chance of never having to use that strength. Above all, we must realize that no arsenal or no weapon in the arsenals of the world is so formidable as the will and moral courage of free men and women. It is a weapon our adversaries in today's world do not have. It is a weapon that we as Americans do have. Let that be understood by those who practice terrorism and prey upon their neighbors. I'm told that tens of thousands of prayer meetings are being held on this day, and for that I'm deeply grateful. We are a nation under God, and I believe God intended for us to be free. It would be fitting and good, I think, if on each Inaugural Day in future years it should be declared a day of prayer.

This is the first time in our history that this ceremony has been held, as you've been told, on the West Front of the Capitol. Standing here, one faces a magnificent vista, opening up on the city's special beauty and history. At the end of this open mall are those shrines to the giants on whose shoulders we stand.

Directly in front of me, the monument to a monumental man, George Washington, father of our country. A man of humility who came to greatness reluctantly. He led Americans out of revolutionary victory into infant nationhood. Off to one side, the stately memorial to Thomas Jefferson. The Declaration of Independence flames with his eloquence. And then, beyond the Reflecting Pool, the dignified columns of the Lincoln Memorial. Whoever would understand in his heart the meaning of America will find it in the life of Abraham Lincoln.

Beyond those monuments to heroism is the Potomac River, and on the far shore the sloping hills of Arlington National Cemetery, with its row upon row of simple white markers bearing crosses or Stars of David. They add up to only a tiny fraction of the price that has been paid for our freedom. Each one of those markers is a monument to the kind of hero I spoke of earlier. Their lives ended in places called Belleau Wood, the Argonne, Omaha Beach, Salerno, and halfway around the world on Guadalcanal, Tarawa, Pork Chop Hill, the Chosin Reservoir, and in a hundred rice paddies and jungles of a place called Vietnam.

Under one such marker lies a young man, Martin Treptow, who left his job in a small town barbershop in 1917 to go to France with the famed Rainbow Division. There, on the western front, he was killed trying to carry a message between battalions under heavy artillery fire.

We're told that on his body was found a diary. On the flyleaf under the heading "My Pledge," he had written these words: "America must win this war. Therefore I will work, I will save, I will sacrifice, I will endure, I will fight cheerfully and do my utmost, as if the issue of the whole struggle depended on me alone."

The crisis we are facing today does not require of us the kind of sacrifice that Martin Treptow and so many thousands of others were called upon to make. It does require, however, our best effort and our willingness to believe in ourselves and to believe in our capacity to perform great deeds, to believe that together with God's help we can and will resolve the problems which now confront us.

And after all, why shouldn't we believe that? We are Americans.

God bless you, and thank you.

The March of Freedom and Democracy

> *On June 8, 1982, Ronald Reagan gave this speech in London in front of the United Kingdom's House of Parliament. He predicted that Marxism-Leninism would be discarded to the "ash-heap of history."*

My Lord Chancellor, Mr. Speaker:

The journey of which this visit forms a part is a long one. Already it has taken me to two great cities of the West, Rome and Paris, and to the economic summit at Versailles. And there, once again, our sister democracies have proved that even in a time of severe economic strain, free peoples can work together freely and voluntarily to address problems as serious as inflation, unemployment, trade, and economic development in a spirit of cooperation and solidarity.

Other milestones lie ahead. Later this week, in Germany, we and our NATO allies will discuss measures for our joint defense and America's latest initiatives for a more peaceful, secure world through arms reductions.

Each stop of this trip is important, but among them all, this moment occupies a special place in my heart and in the hearts of my countrymen – a moment of kinship and homecoming in these hallowed halls.

Speaking for all Americans, I want to say how very much at home we feel in your house. Every American would, because this is, as we have been so eloquently told, one of democracy's shrines. Here the rights of free people and the processes of representation have been debated and refined.

It has been said that an institution is the lengthening shadow of a man. This institution is the lengthening shadow of all the men and women who have sat here and all those who have voted to send representatives here.

This is my second visit to Great Britain as President of the United States. My first opportunity to stand on British soil occurred almost a year and a half ago when your Prime Minister graciously hosted a diplomatic dinner at the British Embassy in Washington. Mrs. Thatcher said then that she hoped I was not distressed to find staring down at me from the grand staircase a portrait of His Royal Majesty King George III. She suggested it was best to let bygones be bygones, and in view of our two countries' remarkable friendship in succeeding years, she added that most Englishmen today would agree with Thomas Jefferson that "a little rebellion now and then is a very good thing." [Laughter]

Well, from here I will go to Bonn and then Berlin, where there stands a grim symbol of power untamed. The Berlin Wall, that dreadful gray gash across the city, is in its third decade. It is the fitting signature of the regime that built it.

And a few hundred kilometers behind the Berlin Wall, there is another symbol. In the center of Warsaw, there is a sign that notes the distances to two capitals. In one direction it points toward Moscow. In the other it points toward Brussels, headquarters of Western Europe's tangible unity. The marker says that the distances from Warsaw to Moscow and Warsaw to Brussels are equal. The sign makes this point: Poland is not East or West. Poland is at the center of European civilization. It has contributed mightily to that civilization. It is doing so today by being magnificently unreconciled to oppression.

Poland's struggle to be Poland and to secure the basic rights we often take for granted demonstrates why we dare not take those rights for granted. Gladstone, defending the Reform Bill of 1866, declared, "You cannot fight against the future. Time is on our side." It was easier to believe in the march of democracy in Gladstone's day – in that high noon of Victorian optimism.

We're approaching the end of a bloody century plagued by a terrible political invention – totalitarianism. Optimism comes less easily today, not because democracy is less vigorous, but because democracy's enemies have refined their instruments of repression. Yet optimism is in order, because day by day democracy is proving itself to be a not-at-all-fragile flower. From Stettin on the Baltic to Varna on the Black Sea, the regimes planted by totalitarianism have had more than 30 years to establish their legitimacy. But none – not one regime – has yet been able to risk free elections. Regimes planted by bayonets do not take root.

The strength of the Solidarity movement in Poland demonstrates the truth told in an underground joke in the Soviet Union. It is that the Soviet Union would remain a one-party nation even if an opposition party were permitted, because everyone would join the opposition party. [Laughter]

America's time as a player on the stage of world history has been brief. I think understanding this fact has always made you patient with your younger cousins – well, not always patient. I do recall that on one occasion, Sir Winston Churchill said in exasperation about one of our most distinguished diplomats: "He is the only case I know of a bull who carries his china shop with him." [Laughter]

But witty as Sir Winston was, he also had that special attribute of great statesmen – the gift of vision, the willingness to see the future based on the experience of the past. It is this sense of history, this understanding of the past that I want to talk with you about today, for it is in remembering what we share of the past that our two nations can make common cause for the future.

We have not inherited an easy world. If developments like the Industrial Revolution, which began here in England, and the gifts of science and technology have made life much easier for us, they have also made it more dangerous. There are threats now to our freedom, indeed to our very existence, that other generations could never even have imagined.

There is first the threat of global war. No President, no Congress, no Prime Minister, no Parliament can spend a day entirely free of this threat. And I don't have to tell you that in today's world the existence of nuclear weapons could mean, if not the extinction of mankind, then surely the end of civilization as we know it. That's why negotiations on intermediate-range nuclear forces now underway in Europe and the START talks – Strategic Arms Reduction Talks – which will begin later this month, are not just critical to American or Western policy; they are critical to mankind. Our commitment to early success in these negotiations is firm and unshakable, and our purpose is clear: reducing the risk of war by reducing the means of waging war on both sides.

At the same time there is a threat posed to human freedom by the enormous power of the modern state. History teaches the dangers of government that overreaches – political control taking precedence over free economic growth, secret police, mindless bureaucracy, all combining to stifle individual excellence and personal freedom.

Now, I'm aware that among us here and throughout Europe there is legitimate disagreement over the extent to which the public sector should play a role in a nation's economy and life. But on one point all of us are united – our abhorrence of dictatorship in all its forms, but most particularly totalitarianism and the terrible inhumanities it has caused in our time – the great purge, Auschwitz and Dachau, the Gulag, and Cambodia.

Historians looking back at our time will note the consistent restraint and peaceful intentions of the West. They will note that it was the democracies who refused to use the threat of their nuclear monopoly in the forties and early fifties for territorial or imperial gain. Had that nuclear monopoly been in the hands of the Communist world, the map of Europe – indeed, the world – would look very different today. And certainly they will note it was not the democracies that invaded Afghanistan or suppressed Polish Solidarity or used chemical and toxin warfare in Afghanistan and Southeast Asia.

If history teaches anything it teaches self-delusion in the face of unpleasant facts is folly. We see around us today the marks of our terrible dilemma – predictions of doomsday, antinuclear demonstrations, an arms race in which the West must, for its own protection, be an unwilling participant. At the same time we see totalitarian forces in the world who seek subversion and conflict around the globe to further their barbarous assault on the human spirit. What, then, is our course? Must civilization perish in a hail of fiery atoms? Must freedom wither in a quiet, deadening accommodation with totalitarian evil?

Sir Winston Churchill refused to accept the inevitability of war or even that it was imminent. He said, "I do not believe that Soviet Russia desires war. What they desire is the fruits of war and the indefinite expansion of their power and doctrines. But what we have to consider here today while time remains is the permanent prevention of war and the establishment of conditions of freedom and democracy as rapidly as possible in all countries."

Well, this is precisely our mission today: to preserve freedom as well as peace. It may not be easy to see; but I believe we live now at a turning point.

In an ironic sense Karl Marx was right. We are witnessing today a great revolutionary crisis, a crisis where the demands of the economic order are conflicting directly with those of the political order. But the crisis is happening not in the free, non-Marxist West, but in the home of Marxist-Leninism, the Soviet Union. It is the Soviet Union that runs against the tide of history by denying human freedom and human dignity to its citizens. It also is in deep economic difficulty. The rate of growth in the national product has been steadily declining since the fifties and is less than half of what it was then.

The dimensions of this failure are astounding: A country which employs one-fifth of its population in agriculture is unable to feed its own people. Were it not for the private sector, the tiny private sector tolerated in Soviet agriculture, the country might be on the brink of famine. These private plots occupy a bare 3 percent of the arable land but account for nearly one-quarter of Soviet farm output and nearly one-third of meat products and vegetables. Overcentralized, with little or no incentives, year after year the Soviet system pours its best resource into the making of instruments of destruction. The constant shrinkage of economic growth combined with the growth of military production is putting a heavy strain on the Soviet people. What we see here is a political structure that no longer corresponds to its economic base, a society where productive forces are hampered by political ones.

The decay of the Soviet experiment should come as no surprise to us. Wherever the comparisons have been made between free and closed societies – West Germany and East Germany, Austria and Czechoslovakia, Malaysia and Vietnam – it is the democratic countries what are prosperous and responsive to the needs of their people. And one of the simple but overwhelming facts of our time is this: Of all the millions of refugees we've seen in the modern world, their flight is always away from, not toward the Communist world. Today on the NATO line, our military forces face east to prevent a possible invasion. On the other side of the line, the Soviet forces also face east to prevent their people from leaving.

The hard evidence of totalitarian rule has caused in mankind an uprising of the intellect and will. Whether it is the growth of the new schools of economics in America or England or the appearance of the so-called new philosophers in France, there is one unifying thread running through the intellectual work of these groups – rejection of the arbitrary power of the state, the refusal to subordinate the rights of the individual to the superstate, the realization that collectivism stifles all the best human impulses.

Since the exodus from Egypt, historians have written of those who sacrificed and struggled for freedom – the stand at Thermopylae, the revolt of Spartacus, the storming of the Bastille, the Warsaw uprising in World War II. More recently we've seen evidence of this same human impulse in one of the developing nations in Central America. For months and months the world news media covered the fighting in El Salvador. Day after day we were treated to stories and film slanted toward the brave freedom-fighters battling oppressive government forces in behalf of the silent, suffering people of that tortured country.

And then one day those silent, suffering people were offered a chance to vote, to choose the kind of government they wanted. Suddenly the freedom-fighters in the hills were exposed for what they really are – Cuban-backed guerrillas who want power for themselves, and their backers, not democracy for the people. They threatened death to any who voted, and destroyed hundreds of buses and trucks to keep the people from getting to the polling places. But on election day, the people of El Salvador, an unprecedented 1.4 million of them, braved ambush and gunfire, and trudged for miles to vote for freedom.

They stood for hours in the hot sun waiting for their turn to vote. Members of our Congress who went there as observers told me of a women who was wounded by rifle fire on the way to the polls, who refused to leave the line to have her wound treated until after she had voted. A grandmother, who had been told by the guerrillas she would be killed when she returned from the polls, and she told the guerrillas, "You can kill me, you can kill my family, kill my neighbors, but you can't kill us all." The real freedom-fighters of El Salvador turned out to be the people of that country – the young, the old, the in-between.

Strange, but in my own country there's been little if any news coverage of that war since the election. Now, perhaps they'll say it's – well, because there are newer struggles now.

On distant islands in the South Atlantic young men are fighting for Britain. And, yes, voices have been raised protesting their sacrifice for lumps of rock and earth so far away. But those young men aren't fighting for mere real estate. They fight for a cause – for the belief that armed aggression must not be allowed to succeed, and the people must participate in the decisions of government – [applause] – the decisions of government under the rule of law. If there had been firmer support for that principle some 45 years ago, perhaps our generation wouldn't have suffered the bloodletting of World War II.

In the Middle East now the guns sound once more, this time in Lebanon, a country that for too long has had to endure the tragedy of civil war, terrorism, and foreign intervention and occupation. The fighting in Lebanon on the part of all parties must stop, and Israel should bring its forces home. But this is not enough. We must all work to stamp out the scourge of terrorism that in the Middle East makes war an ever-present threat.

But beyond the troublespots lies a deeper, more positive pattern. Around the world today, the democratic revolution is gathering new strength. In India a critical test has been passed with the peaceful change of governing political parties. In Africa, Nigeria is moving into remarkable and unmistakable ways to build and strengthen its democratic institutions. In the Caribbean and Central America, 16 of 24 countries have freely elected governments. And in the United Nations, 8 of the 10 developing nations which have joined that body in the past 5 years are democracies.

In the Communist world as well, man's instinctive desire for freedom and self-determination surfaces again and again. To be sure, there are grim reminders of how brutally the police state attempts to snuff out this quest for self-rule – 1953 in East Germany, 1956 in Hungary, 1968 in Czechoslovakia, 1981 in Poland. But the struggle continues in Poland. And we know that there are even those who strive and suffer for freedom within the confines of the Soviet Union itself. How we conduct ourselves here in the Western democracies will determine whether this trend continues.

No, democracy is not a fragile flower. Still it needs cultivating. If the rest of this century is to witness the gradual growth of freedom and democratic ideals, we must take actions to assist the campaign for democracy.

Some argue that we should encourage democratic change in right-wing dictatorships, but not in Communist regimes. Well, to accept this preposterous notion – as some well-meaning people have – is to invite the argument that once countries achieve a nuclear capability, they should be allowed an undisturbed reign of terror over their own citizens. We reject this course.

As for the Soviet view, Chairman Brezhnev repeatedly has stressed that the competition of ideas and systems must continue and that this is entirely consistent with relaxation of tensions and peace.

Well, we ask only that these systems begin by living up to their own constitutions, abiding by their own laws, and complying with the international obligations they have undertaken. We ask only for a process, a direction, a basic code of decency, not for an instant transformation.

We cannot ignore the fact that even without our encouragement there has been and will continue to be repeated explosions against repression and dictatorships. The Soviet Union itself is not immune to this reality. Any system is inherently unstable that has no peaceful means to legitimize its leaders. In such cases, the very repressiveness of the state ultimately drives people to resist it, if necessary, by force.

While we must be cautious about forcing the pace of change, we must not hesitate to declare our ultimate objectives and to take concrete actions to move toward them. We must be staunch in our conviction that freedom is not the sole prerogative of a lucky few, but the inalienable and universal right of all human beings. So states the United Nations Universal Declaration of Human Rights, which, among other things, guarantees free elections.

The objective I propose is quite simple to state: to foster the infrastructure of democracy, the system of a free press, unions, political parties, universities, which allows a people to choose their own way to develop their own culture, to reconcile their own differences through peaceful means.

This is not cultural imperialism, it is providing the means for genuine self-determination and protection for diversity. Democracy already flourishes in countries with very different cultures and historical experiences. It would be cultural condescension, or worse, to say that any people prefer dictatorship to democracy. Who would voluntarily choose not to have the right to vote, decide to purchase government propaganda handouts instead of independent newspapers, prefer government to worker-controlled unions, opt for land to be owned by the state instead of those who till it, want government repression of religious liberty, a single political party instead of a free choice, a rigid cultural orthodoxy instead of democratic tolerance and diversity?

Since 1917 the Soviet Union has given covert political training and assistance to Marxist-Leninists in many countries. Of course, it also has promoted the use of violence and subversion by these same forces. Over the past several decades, West European and other Social Democrats, Christian Democrats, and leaders have offered open assistance to fraternal, political, and social institutions to bring about peaceful and democratic progress. Appropriately, for a vigorous new democracy, the Federal Republic of Germany's political foundations have become a major force in this effort.

We in America now intend to take additional steps, as many of our allies have already done, toward realizing this same goal. The chairmen and other leaders of the national Republican and Democratic Party organizations are initiating a study with the bipartisan American political foundation to determine how the United States can best contribute as a nation to the global campaign for democracy now gathering force. They will have the cooperation of congressional leaders of both parties, along with representatives of business, labor, and other major institutions in our society. I look forward to receiving their recommendations and to working with these institutions and the Congress in the common task of strengthening democracy throughout the world.

It is time that we committed ourselves as a nation – in both the pubic and private sectors – to assisting democratic development.

We plan to consult with leaders of other nations as well. There is a proposal before the Council of Europe to invite parliamentarians from democratic countries to a meeting next year in Strasbourg. That prestigious gathering could consider ways to help democratic political movements.

This November in Washington there will take place an international meeting on free elections. And next spring there will be a conference of world authorities on constitutionalism and self-government hosted by the Chief Justice of the United States. Authorities from a number of developing and developed countries – judges, philosophers, and politicians with practical experience – have agreed to explore how to turn principle into practice and further the rule of law.

At the same time, we invite the Soviet Union to consider with us how the competition of ideas and values – which it is committed to support – can be conducted on a peaceful and reciprocal basis. For example, I am prepared to offer President Brezhnev an opportunity to speak to the American people on our television if he will allow me the same opportunity with the Soviet people. We also suggest that panels of our newsmen periodically appear on each other's television to discuss major events.

Now, I don't wish to sound overly optimistic, yet the Soviet Union is not immune from the reality of what is going on in the world. It has happened in the past – a small ruling elite either mistakenly attempts to ease domestic unrest through greater repression and foreign adventure, or it chooses a wiser course. It begins to allow its people a voice in their own destiny. Even if this latter process is not realized soon, I believe the renewed strength of the democratic movement, complemented by a global campaign for freedom, will strengthen the prospects for arms control and a world at peace.

I have discussed on other occasions, including my address on May 9th, the elements of Western policies toward the Soviet Union to safeguard our interests and protect the peace. What I am describing now is a plan and a hope for the long term – the march of freedom and democracy which will leave Marxism-Leninism on the ash-heap of history as it has left other tyrannies which stifle the freedom and muzzle the self-expression of the people. And that's why we must continue our efforts to strengthen

NATO even as we move forward with our Zero-Option initiative in the negotiations on intermediate-range forces and our proposal for a one-third reduction in strategic ballistic missile warheads.

Our military strength is a prerequisite to peace, but let it be clear we maintain this strength in the hope it will never be used, for the ultimate determinant in the struggle that's now going on in the world will not be bombs and rockets, but a test of wills and ideas, a trial of spiritual resolve, the values we hold, the beliefs we cherish, the ideals to which we are dedicated.

The British people know that, given strong leadership, time and a little bit of hope, the forces of good ultimately rally and triumph over evil. Here among you is the cradle of self-government, the Mother of Parliaments. Here is the enduring greatness of the British contribution to mankind, the great civilized ideas: individual liberty, representative government, and the rule of law under God.

I've often wondered about the shyness of some of us in the West about standing for these ideals that have done so much to ease the plight of man and the hardships of our imperfect world. This reluctance to use those vast resources at our command reminds me of the elderly lady whose home was bombed in the Blitz. As the rescuers moved about, they found a bottle of brandy she'd stored behind the staircase, which was all that was left standing. And since she was barely conscious, one of the workers pulled the cork to give her a taste of it. She came around immediately and said, "Here now – there now, put it back. That's for emergencies." [Laughter]

Well, the emergency is upon us. Let us be shy no longer. Let us go to our strength. Let us offer hope. Let us tell the world that a new age is not only possible but probable.

During the dark days of the Second World War, when this island was incandescent with courage, Winston Churchill exclaimed about Britain's adversaries, "What kind of a people do they think we are?" Well, Britain's adversaries found out what extraordinary people the British are. But all the democracies paid a terrible price for allowing the dictators to underestimate us. We dare not make that mistake again. So, let us ask ourselves, "What kind of people do we think we are?" And let us answer, "Free people, worthy of freedom and determined not only to remain so but to help others gain their freedom as well."

Sir Winston led his people to great victory in war and then lost an election just as the fruits of victory were about to be enjoyed. But he left office honorably, and, as it turned out, temporarily, knowing that the liberty of his people was more important than the fate of any single leader. History recalls his greatness in ways no dictator will ever know. And he left us a message of hope for the future, as timely now as when he first uttered it, as opposition leader in the Commons nearly 27 years ago, when he said, "When we look back on all the perils through which we have passed and at the mighty foes that we have laid low and all the dark and deadly designs that we have frustrated, why should we fear for our future? We have," he said, "come safely through the worst."

Well, the task I've set forth will long outlive our own generation. But together, we too have come through the worst. Let us now begin a major effort to secure the best — a crusade for freedom that will engage the faith and fortitude of the next generation. For the sake of peace and justice, let us move toward a world in which all people are at last free to determine their own destiny.

Thank you.

The "Evil Empire" Speech

*Reagan used the phrase "evil empire" at the end of his speech to
describe the Soviet Union at the Annual Convention of the National
Association of Evangelicals in Orlando, Florida, on March 8, 1983.*

Reverend clergy all, Senator Hawkins, distinguished members of
the Florida congressional delegation, and all of you:

I can't tell you how you have warmed my heart with your welcome.
I'm delighted to be here today.

Those of you in the National Association of Evangelicals are known
for your spiritual and humanitarian work. And I would be especially remiss
if I didn't discharge right now one personal debt of gratitude. Thank you
for your prayers. Nancy and I have felt their presence many times in
many ways. And believe me, for us they've made all the difference.

The other day in the East Room of the White House at a meeting
there, someone asked me whether I was aware of all the people out there
who were praying for the President. And I had to say, "Yes, I am. I've felt
it. I believe in intercessionary prayer." But I couldn't help but say to that
questioner after he'd asked the question that – or at least say to them
that if sometimes when he was praying he got a busy signal, it was just
me in there ahead of him. [Laughter] I think I understand how Abraham
Lincoln felt when he said, "I have been driven many times to my knees
by the overwhelming conviction that I had nowhere else to go."

From the joy and the good feeling of this conference, I go to a political
reception. [Laughter] Now, I don't know why, but that bit of scheduling
reminds me of a story – [laughter] – which I'll share with you.

An evangelical minister and a politician arrived at Heaven's gate
one day together. And St. Peter, after doing all the necessary formalities,
took them in hand to show them where their quarters would be. And he
took them to a small, single room with a bed, a chair, and a table and said
this was for the clergyman. And the politician was a little worried about
what might be in store for him. And he couldn't believe it then when St.
Peter stopped in front of a beautiful mansion with lovely grounds, many
servants, and told him that these would be his quarters.

And he couldn't help but ask, he said, "But wait, how – there's
something wrong – how do I get this mansion while that good and holy
man only gets a single room?" And St. Peter said, "You have to understand

how things are up here. We've got thousands and thousands of clergy. You're the first politician who ever made it." [Laughter]

But I don't want to contribute to a stereotype. [Laughter] So, I tell you there are a great many God-fearing, dedicated, noble men and women in public life, present company included. And, yes, we need your help to keep us ever mindful of the ideas and the principles that brought us into the public arena in the first place. The basis of those ideals and principles is a commitment to freedom and personal liberty that, itself, is grounded in the much deeper realization that freedom prospers only where the blessings of God are avidly sought and humbly accepted.

The American experiment in democracy rests on this insight. Its discovery was the great triumph of our Founding Fathers, voiced by William Penn when he said: "If we will not be governed by God, we must be governed by tyrants." Explaining the inalienable rights of men, Jefferson said, "The God who gave us life, gave us liberty at the same time." And it was George Washington who said that "of all the dispositions and habits which lead to political prosperity, religion and morality are indispensable supports."

And finally, that shrewdest of all observers of American democracy, Alexis de Tocqueville, put it eloquently after he had gone on a search for the secret of America's greatness and genius – and he said: "Not until I went into the churches of America and heard her pulpits aflame with righteousness did I understand the greatness and the genius of America. . . . America is good. And if America ever ceases to be good, America will cease to be great."

Well, I'm pleased to be here today with you who are keeping America great by keeping her good. Only through your work and prayers and those of millions of others can we hope to survive this perilous century and keep alive this experiment in liberty, this last, best hope of man.

I want you to know that this administration is motivated by a political philosophy that sees the greatness of America in you, her people, and in your families, churches, neighborhoods, communities – the institutions that foster and nourish values like concern for others and respect for the rule of law under God.

Now, I don't have to tell you that this puts us in opposition to, or at least out of step with, a prevailing attitude of many who have turned to a modern-day secularism, discarding the tried and time-tested values upon which our very civilization is based. No matter how well intentioned, their value system is radically different from that of most Americans. And while they proclaim that they're freeing us from superstitions of the past, they've taken upon themselves the job of superintending us by government rule and regulation. Sometimes their voices are louder than ours, but they are not yet a majority.

An example of that vocal superiority is evident in a controversy now going on in Washington. And since I'm involved, I've been waiting to hear from the parents of young America. How far are they willing to go in giving to government their prerogatives as parents?

Let me state the case as briefly and simply as I can. An organization of citizens, sincerely motivated and deeply concerned about the increase in illegitimate births and abortions involving girls well below the age of consent, sometime ago established a nationwide network of clinics to offer help to these girls and, hopefully, alleviate this situation. Now, again, let me say, I do not fault their intent. However, in their well-intentioned effort, these clinics have decided to provide advice and birth control drugs and devices to underage girls without the knowledge of their parents.

For some years now, the Federal Government has helped with funds to subsidize these clinics. In providing for this, the Congress decreed that every effort would be made to maximize parental participation. Nevertheless, the drugs and devices are prescribed without getting parental consent or giving notification after they've done so. Girls termed "sexually active" – and that has replaced the word "promiscuous" – are given this help in order to prevent illegitimate birth or abortion.

Well, we have ordered clinics receiving Federal funds to notify the parents such help has been given. One of the Nation's leading newspapers has created the term "squeal rule" in editorializing against us for doing this, and we're being criticized for violating the privacy of young people. A judge has recently granted an injunction against an enforcement of our rule. I've watched TV panel shows discuss this issue, seen columnists pontificating on our error, but no one seems to mention morality as playing a part in the subject of sex.

Is all of Judeo-Christian tradition wrong? Are we to believe that something so sacred can be looked upon as a purely physical thing with no potential for emotional and psychological harm? And isn't it the parents' right to give counsel and advice to keep their children from making mistakes that may affect their entire lives?

Many of us in government would like to know what parents think about this intrusion in their family by government. We're going to fight in the courts. The right of parents and the rights of family take precedence over those of Washington-based bureaucrats and social engineers.

But the fight against parental notification is really only one example of many attempts to water down traditional values and even abrogate the original terms of American democracy. Freedom prospers when religion is vibrant and the rule of law under God is acknowledged. When our Founding Fathers passed the first amendment, they sought to protect churches from government interference. They never intended to construct a wall of hostility between government and the concept of religious belief itself.

The evidence of this permeates our history and our government. The Declaration of Independence mentions the Supreme Being no less than four times. "In God We Trust" is engraved on our coinage. The Supreme Court opens its proceedings with a religious invocation. And the Members of Congress open their sessions with a prayer. I just happen to believe the schoolchildren of the United States are entitled to the same privileges as Supreme Court Justices and Congressmen.

Last year, I sent the Congress a constitutional amendment to restore prayer to public schools. Already this session, there's growing bipartisan support for the amendment, and I am calling on the Congress to act speedily to pass it and to let our children pray.

Perhaps some of you read recently about the Lubbock school case, where a judge actually ruled that it was unconstitutional for a school district to give equal treatment to religious and nonreligious student groups, even when the group meetings were being held during the students' own time. The first amendment never intended to require government to discriminate against religious speech.

Senators Denton and Hatfield have proposed legislation in the Congress on the whole question of prohibiting discrimination against religious forms of student speech. Such legislation could go far to restore freedom of religious speech for public school students. And I hope the Congress considers these bills quickly. And with your help, I think it's possible we could also get the constitutional amendment through the Congress this year.

More than a decade ago, a Supreme Court decision literally wiped off the books of 50 States statutes protecting the rights of unborn children.

Abortion on demand now takes the lives of up to 1 1/2 million unborn children a year. Human life legislation ending this tragedy will some day pass the Congress, and you and I must never rest until it does. Unless and until it can be proven that the unborn child is not a living entity, then its right to life, liberty, and the pursuit of happiness must be protected.

You may remember that when abortion on demand began, many, and, indeed, I'm sure many of you, warned that the practice would lead to a decline in respect for human life, that the philosophical premises used to justify abortion on demand would ultimately be used to justify other attacks on the sacredness of human life – infanticide or mercy killing. Tragically enough, those warnings proved all too true. Only last year a court permitted the death by starvation of a handicapped infant.

I have directed the Health and Human Services Department to make clear to every health care facility in the United States that the Rehabilitation Act of 1973 protects all handicapped persons against discrimination based on handicaps, including infants. And we have taken the further step of requiring that each and every recipient of Federal funds who provides health care services to infants must post and keep posted in a conspicuous place a notice stating that "discriminatory failure to feed and care for handicapped infants in this facility is prohibited by Federal law." It also lists a 24-hour, toll-free number so that nurses and others may report violations in time to save the infant's life.

In addition, recent legislation introduced in the Congress by Representative Henry Hyde of Illinois not only increases restrictions on publicly financed abortions, it also addresses this whole problem of infanticide. I urge the Congress to begin hearings and to adopt legislation that will protect the right of life to all children, including the disabled or handicapped.

Now, I'm sure that you must get discouraged at times, but you've done better than you know, perhaps. There's a great spiritual awakening in America, a renewal of the traditional values that have been the bedrock of America's goodness and greatness.

One recent survey by a Washington-based research council concluded that Americans were far more religious than the people of other nations; 95 percent of those surveyed expressed a belief in God and a huge majority believed the Ten Commandments had real meaning in their lives. And another study has found that an overwhelming majority of Americans disapprove of adultery, teenage sex, pornography, abortion, and hard drugs.

And this same study showed a deep reverence for the importance of family ties and religious belief.

I think the items that we've discussed here today must be a key part of the Nation's political agenda. For the first time the Congress is openly and seriously debating and dealing with the prayer and abortion issues – and that's enormous progress right there. I repeat: America is in the midst of a spiritual awakening and a moral renewal. And with your Biblical keynote, I say today, "Yes, let justice roll on like a river, righteousness like a never-failing stream."

Now, obviously, much of this new political and social consensus I've talked about is based on a positive view of American history, one that takes pride in our country's accomplishments and record. But we must never forget that no government schemes are going to perfect man. We know that living in this world means dealing with what philosophers would call the phenomenology of evil or, as theologians would put it, the doctrine of sin.

There is sin and evil in the world, and we're enjoined by Scripture and the Lord Jesus to oppose it with all our might. Our nation, too, has a legacy of evil with which it must deal. The glory of this land has been its capacity for transcending the moral evils of our past. For example, the long struggle of minority citizens for equal rights, once a source of disunity and civil war, is now a point of pride for all Americans. We must never go back. There is no room for racism, anti-Semitism, or other forms of ethnic and racial hatred in this country.

I know that you've been horrified, as have I, by the resurgence of some hate groups preaching bigotry and prejudice. Use the mighty voice of your pulpits and the powerful standing of your churches to denounce and isolate these hate groups in our midst. The commandment given us is clear and simple: "Thou shalt love thy neighbor as thyself."

But whatever sad episodes exist in our past, any objective observer must hold a positive view of American history, a history that has been the story of hopes fulfilled and dreams made into reality. Especially in this century, America has kept alight the torch of freedom, but not just for ourselves but for millions of others around the world.

And this brings me to my final point today. During my first press conference as President, in answer to a direct question, I pointed out that, as good Marxist-Leninists, the Soviet leaders have openly and publicly declared that the only morality they recognize is that which will further their cause, which is world revolution. I think I should point out I was only quoting Lenin, their guiding spirit. who said in 1920 that they repudiate all morality that proceeds from supernatural ideas – that's their name for religion – or ideas that are outside class conceptions. Morality is entirely subordinate to the interests of class war. And everything is moral that is necessary for the annihilation of the old, exploiting social order and for uniting the proletariat.

Well, I think the refusal of many influential people to accept this elementary fact of Soviet doctrine illustrates an historical reluctance to see totalitarian powers for what they are. We saw this phenomenon in the 1930's. We see it too often today.

This doesn't mean we should isolate ourselves and refuse to seek an understanding with them. I intend to do everything I can to persuade them of our peaceful intent, to remind them that it was the West that refused to use its nuclear monopoly in the forties and fifties for territorial gain and which now proposes 50-percent cut in strategic ballistic missiles and the elimination of an entire class of land-based, intermediate-range nuclear missiles.

At the same time, however, they must be made to understand we will never compromise our principles and standards. We will never give away our freedom. We will never abandon our belief in God. And we will never stop searching for a genuine peace. But we can assure none of these things America stands for through the so-called nuclear freeze solutions proposed by some.

The truth is that a freeze now would be a very dangerous fraud, for that is merely the illusion of peace. The reality is that we must find peace through strength.

I would agree to a freeze if only we could freeze the Soviets' global desires. A freeze at current levels of weapons would remove any incentive for the Soviets to negotiate seriously in Geneva and virtually end our chances to achieve the major arms reductions which we have proposed. Instead, they would achieve their objectives through the freeze.

A freeze would reward the Soviet Union for its enormous and unparalleled military buildup. It would prevent the essential and long overdue modernization of United States and allied defenses and would leave our aging forces increasingly vulnerable. And an honest freeze would require extensive prior negotiations on the systems and numbers to be limited and on the measures to ensure effective verification and compliance. And the kind of a freeze that has been suggested would be virtually impossible to verify. Such a major effort would divert us completely from our current negotiations on achieving substantial reductions.

A number of years ago, I heard a young father, a very prominent young man in the entertainment world, addressing a tremendous gathering in California. It was during the time of the cold war, and communism and our own way of life were very much on people's minds. And he was speaking to that subject. And suddenly, though, I heard him saying, "I love my little girls more than anything..." And I said to myself, "Oh, no, don't. You can't – don't say that." But I had underestimated him. He went on: "I would rather see my little girls die now, still believing in God, than have them grow up under communism and one day die no longer believing in God."

There were thousands of young people in that audience. They came to their feet with shouts of joy. They had instantly recognized the profound truth in what he had said, with regard to the physical and the soul and what was truly important.

Yes, let us pray for the salvation of all of those who live in that totalitarian darkness – pray they will discover the joy of knowing God. But until they do, let us be aware that while they preach the supremacy of the state, declare its omnipotence over individual man, and predict its eventual domination of all peoples on the Earth, they are the locus of evil in the modern world.

It was C. S. Lewis who, in his unforgettable "Screwtape Letters," wrote: "The greatest evil is not done now in those sordid `dens of crime' that Dickens loved to paint. It is not even done in concentration camps and labor camps. In those we see its final result. But it is conceived and ordered (moved, seconded, carried and minuted) in clear, carpeted, warmed, and well-lighted offices, by quiet men with white collars and cut fingernails and smooth-shaven cheeks who do not need to raise their voice."

Well, because these "quiet men" do not "raise their voices," because they sometimes speak in soothing tones of brotherhood and peace, because, like other dictators before them, they're always making "their final territorial demand," some would have us accept them at their word and accommodate ourselves to their aggressive impulses. But if history teaches anything, it teaches that simple-minded appeasement or wishful thinking about our adversaries is folly. It means the betrayal of our past, the squandering of our freedom.

So, I urge you to speak out against those who would place the United States in a position of military and moral inferiority. You know, I've always believed that old Screwtape reserved his best efforts for those of you in the church. So, in your discussions of the nuclear freeze proposals, I urge you to beware the temptation of pride – the temptation of blithely declaring yourselves above it all and label both sides equally at fault, to ignore the facts of history and the aggressive impulses of an evil empire, to simply call the arms race a giant misunderstanding and thereby remove yourself from the struggle between right and wrong and good and evil.

I ask you to resist the attempts of those who would have you withhold your support for our efforts, this administration's efforts, to keep America strong and free, while we negotiate real and verifiable reductions in the world's nuclear arsenals and one day, with God's help, their total elimination.

While America's military strength is important, let me add here that I've always maintained that the struggle now going on for the world will never be decided by bombs or rockets, by armies or military might. The real crisis we face today is a spiritual one; at root, it is a test of moral will and faith.

Whittaker Chambers, the man whose own religious conversion made him a witness to one of the terrible traumas of our time, the Hiss-Chambers case, wrote that the crisis of the Western World exists to the degree in which the West is indifferent to God, the degree to which it collaborates in communism's attempt to make man stand alone without God. And then he said, for Marxism-Leninism is actually the second oldest faith, first proclaimed in the Garden of Eden with the words of temptation, "Ye shall be as gods."

The Western World can answer this challenge, he wrote, "but only provided that its faith in God and the freedom He enjoins is as great as communism's faith in Man."

I believe we shall rise to the challenge. I believe that communism is another sad, bizarre chapter in human history whose last pages even now are being written. I believe this because the source of our strength in the quest for human freedom is not material, but spiritual. And because it knows no limitation, it must terrify and ultimately triumph over those who would enslave their fellow man. For in the words of Isaiah: "He giveth power to the faint; and to them that have no might He increased strength. . . . But they that wait upon the Lord shall renew their strength;

they shall mount up with wings as eagles; they shall run, and not be weary.
. . ."

Yes, change your world. One of our Founding Fathers, Thomas Paine, said, "We have it within our power to begin the world over again." We can do it, doing together what no one church could do by itself.

God bless you, and thank you very much.

Creators of the Future

Reagan spoke at the annual meeting of the Conservative Political Action Committee on March 8, 1985.

Thank you all very much. Thank you Vice Chairman [of the American Conservative Union James A.] Linen, for those very kind words. I'm grateful to the American Conservative Union, Young Americans for Freedom, *National Review, Human Events,* for organizing this wonderful evening. When you work in the White House, you don't get to see your old friends as much as you'd like. And I always see the Conservative Political Action Conference speech as my opportunity to "dance with the one that brung ya."

There's so much I want to talk about tonight. I've been thinking, in the weeks since the inauguration, that we are at an especially dramatic turning point in American history. And just putting it all together in my mind, I've been reviewing the elements that have led to this moment.

Ever since F.D.R. and the New Deal, the opposition party, and particularly those of a liberal persuasion, have dominated the political debate. Their ideas were new; they had momentum; they captured the imagination of the American people. The left held sway for a long time. There was a right, but it was, by the '40s and '50s, diffuse and scattered, without a unifying voice.

But in 1964 came a voice in the wilderness-Barry Goldwater; the great Barry Goldwater, the first major party candidate of our time who was a true-blue, undiluted conservative. He spoke from principle, and he offered vision. Freedom-he spoke of freedom: freedom from the government's increasing demands on the family purse, freedom from the government's increasing usurpation of individual rights and responsibilities, freedom from the leaders who told us the price of world peace is continued acquiescence to totalitarianism. He was ahead of his time. When he ran for President, he won six states and lost 44. But his candidacy worked as a precursor of things to come.

A new movement was stirring. And in the 1960's Young Americans for Freedom is born; *National Review* gains readership and prestige in the intellectual community; *Human Events* becomes a major voice on the cutting edge. In the '70s the anti-tax movement begins. Actually, it was much more than an anti-tax movement, just as the Boston Tea Party was much more than an anti-tax initiative. In the late '70s Proposition 13 and the Sagebrush Rebellion; in 1980, for the first time in 28 years, a

Republican Senate is elected; so, may I say, is a conservative President. In 1984 that conservative administration is reselected in a 49-state sweep. And the day the votes came in, I thought of Walt Whitman: "I hear America singing."

This great turn from left to right was not just a case of the pendulum swinging: First, the left hold sway and then the right, and here comes the left again. The truth is, conservative thought is no longer over here on the right: it's the mainstream now.

And the tide of history is moving irresistibly in our direction. Why? Because the other side is virtually bankrupt of ideas. It has nothing more to say, nothing to add to the debate. It has spent its intellectual capital, such as it was, and it has done its deeds.

Now, we're not in power because they failed to gain electoral support over the past 50 years. They did win support. And the result was chaos, weakness, and drift. Ultimately, though, their failures yielded one great thing-us guys. We in this room are not simply profiting from their bankruptcy; we are where we are because we're winning the contest of ideas. In fact, in the past decade, all of a sudden, quietly, mysteriously, the Republican party has become the party of ideas.

We became the party of the most brilliant and dynamic young minds. I remember them, just a few years ago, running around scrawling Laffer curves on table napkins, going to symposia and talking about how social programs did not eradicate poverty, but entrenched it; writing studies on why the latest weird and unnatural idea from the social engineers is weird and unnatural. You were there. They were your ideas, your symposia, your books, and usually somebody else's table napkins.

All of a sudden, Republicans were not defenders of the status quo but creators of the future. They were looking at tomorrow with all the single-mindedness of an inventor. In fact, they reminded me of the American inventors of the 19th and 20th centuries who filled the world with light and recorded sound.

The new conservatives made anew the connection between economic justice and economic growth. Growth in the economy would not only create jobs and paychecks, they said; it would enhance familial stability and encourage a healthy optimism about the future. Lower those tax rates, they said, and let the economy become the engine of our dreams. Pull back regulations, and encourage free and open competition. Let the men and women of the marketplace decide what they want.

But along with that, perhaps the greatest triumph of modern conservatism has been to stop allowing the left to put the average American on the moral defensive. By average American I mean the good, decent, rambunctious, and creative people who raise the families, go to church, and help out when the local library holds a fundraiser; people who have a stake in the community because they are the community.

These people had held true to certain beliefs and principles that for 20 years the intelligentsia were telling us were hopelessly out of date, utterly trite, and reactionary. You want prayer in the schools? How primitive, they said. You oppose abortion? How oppressive, how anti-modern. The normal was portrayed as eccentric, and only the abnormal was worthy of emulation. The irreverent was celebrated, but only irreverence about certain things: irreverence toward, say, organized religion, yes; irreverence toward established liberalism, not too much of that. They celebrated their courage in taking on safe targets and patted each other on the back for slinging stones at a confused Goliath, who was too demoralized and really too good to fight back. But now one simply senses it. The American people are no longer on the defensive. I believe the conservative movement deserves some credit for this. You spoke for the permanent against the merely prevalent, and ultimately you prevailed.

I believe we conservatives have captured the moment, captured the imagination of the American people. And what now? What are we to do with our success? Well, right now, with conservative thought accepted as mainstream thought and with the people of our country leading the fight to freedom, now we must move.

You remember your Shakespeare: "There is a tide in the affairs of men which, taken at the flood, leads on to fortune. Omitted, all the voyage of their life is bound in shallows and in miseries. On such a full sea are we now afloat. And we must take the current when it serves, or lose our ventures." I spoke in the ·[applause]. It's typical, isn't it? I just quoted a great writer, but as an actor, I get the bow. [Laughter]

I spoke in the State of the Union of a second American revolution, and now is the time to launch that revolution and see that it takes hold . If we move decisively, these years will not be just a passing era of good feeling, not just a few good years, but a true golden age of freedom.

The moment is ours, and we must seize it. There's work to do. We must prolong and protect our growing prosperity so that it doesn't become just a passing phase, a natural adjustment between periods of recession.

We must move further to provide incentives and make America the investment capital of the world.

We must institute a fair tax system and turn the current one on its ear. I believe there is natural support in our country for a simplified tax system, with still lower tax rates but a broader base, with everyone paying their fair share and no more. We must eliminate unproductive tax shelters. Again, there is natural support among Americans, because Americans are a fair-minded people.

We must institute enterprise zones and a lower youth minimum wage so we can revitalize distressed areas and teenagers can get jobs. We're going to take our revolution to the people, all of the people. We're going to go to black Americans and members of all minority groups, and we're going to make our case.

Part of being a revolutionary is knowing that you don't have to acquiesce to the tired, old ideas of the past. One such idea is that the opposition party has black America and minority America locked up, that they own black America. Well, let me tell you, they own nothing but the past. The old alignments are no longer legitimate, if they ever were.

We're going to reach out, and we need your help. Conservatives were brought up to hate deficits, and justifiably so. We've long thought there are two things in Washington that are unbalanced-the budget and the liberals.

But we cannot reduce the deficit by raising taxes . And just so that every "i" is dotted and every "t" is crossed, let me repeat tonight for the benefit of those who never seem to get the message: we will not reduce the deficit by raising taxes. We need more taxes like John McLaughlin [Washington executive editor of *National Review*] needs assertiveness training.

Now, whether government borrows or increases taxes, it will be taking the same amount of money from the private economy, and either way, that's too much. We must bring down government spending. We need a constitutional amendment requiring a balanced budget. It's something that 49 states already require -no reason the federal government should be any different.

We need the line-item veto, which 43 governors have-no reason that the President shouldn't. And we have to cut waste. The Grace commission has identified billions of dollars that are wasted and that we can save.

But the domestic side isn't the only area where we need your help. All of us in this room grew up, or came to adulthood, in a time when the doctrine of Marx and Lenin was coming to divide the world. Ultimately, it came to dominate remorselessly whole parts of it. The Soviet attempt to give legitimacy to its tyranny is expressed in the infamous Brezhnev doctrine, which contends that once a country has fallen into Communist darkness, it can never again be allowed to see the light of freedom.

Well, it occurs to me that history has already begun to repeal that doctrine. It started one day in Grenada. We only did our duty, as a responsible neighbor and a lover of peace, the day we went in and returned the government to the people and rescued our own students. We restored that island to liberty. Yes, it's only a small island, but that's what the world is made of-small islands yearning for freedom.

There's much more to do. Throughout the world the Soviet Union and its agents, client states, and satellites are on the defensive-on the moral defensive, the intellectual defensive, and the political and economic defensive. Freedom movements arise and assert themselves. They're doing so on almost every continent populated by man-in the hills of Afghanistan, in Angola, in Kampuchea, in Central America. In making mention of freedom fighters, all of us are privileged to have in our midst tonight one of the brave commanders who lead the Afghan freedom fighters-Abdul Haq. Abdul Haq, we are with you.

They are our brothers, these freedom fighters, and we owe them our help. I've spoken recently of the freedom fighters of Nicaragua. You know the truth about them. You know who they're fighting and why. They are the moral equal of our Founding Fathers and the brave men and women of the French Resistance. We cannot turn away from them for the struggle here is not right versus left; it is right versus wrong.

Now I am against sending troops to Central America. They are simply not needed. Given a chance and the resources the people of the area can fight their own fight. They have the men and women. They're capable of doing it. They have the people of their country behind them. All they need is our support. All they need is proof that we care as much about the fight for freedom 700 miles from our shores as the Soviets care about the fight against freedom 5,000 miles from theirs. And they need to know that the U.S. supports them with more than just pretty words and good wishes. We need your help on this and I mean each of you-involved active strong and vocal. And we need more.

All of you know that we re researching non-nuclear technologies that may enable us to prevent nuclear ballistic missiles from reaching U.S. soil or that of our allies. I happen to believe -logic forces me to believe- that this new defense system the Strategic Defense Initiative is the most hopeful possibility of our time. Its primary virtue is clear. If anyone ever attacked us Strategic Defense would be there to protect us. It could conceivably save millions of lives.

SDI has been criticized on the grounds that it might upset any chance of an arms control agreement with the Soviets. But SDI is arms control. If SDI is say 80 percent effective then it will make any Soviet attack folly. Even partial success in SDI would strengthen deterrence and keep the peace. And if our SDI research is successful the prospects for real reduction in U.S. and Soviet offensive nuclear forces will be greatly enhanced.

It is said that SDI would deal a blow to the so-called East-West balance of power. Well let's think about that. The Soviets already are investing roughly as much on strategic defenses as they are on their offensive nuclear forces. This could quickly tip the East-West balance if we had no defense of our own. Would a situation of comparable defenses threaten us? No for we're not planning on being the first to use force.

As we strive for our goal of eventual elimination of nuclear weapons, each side would retain a certain amount of defensive-or of, I should say, destructive power-a certain number of missiles. But it would not be in our interest, or theirs, to build more and more of them.

Now, one would think our critics on the left would quickly embrace, or at least be open-minded about a system that promises to reduce the size of nuclear missile forces on both sides and to greatly enhance the prospects for real arms reductions. And yet we hear SDI belittled by some with nicknames, or demagogued with charges that it will bring war to the heavens.

They complain that it won't work, which is odd from people who profess to believe in the perfectibility of man. Machines, after all, are so much easier to manipulate. They say it won't be 100 percent effective, which is odd, since they don't ask for 100 percent effectiveness in their social experiments. They say SDI is only in the research stage and won't be realized in time to change things. To which, as I said last month, the only reply is: then let's get started.

Now, my point here is not to question the motives of others. But it's difficult to understand how critics can object to exploring the possibility of moving away from exclusive reliance upon nuclear weapons. The truth is, I believe that they find it difficult to embrace any idea that breaks with the past, that breaks with consensus thinking and the common establishment wisdom. In short, they find it difficult and frightening to alter the status quo.

And what are we to do when these so-called opinion leaders of an outworn philosophy are out there on television and in the newspapers with their steady drumbeat of doubt and distaste? Well, when all you have to do to win is rely on the good judgment of the American people, then you're in good shape, because the American people have good judgment. I know it isn't becoming of me, but I like to think that maybe 49 of our 50 states displayed that judgment just a few months ago.

What we have to do, all of us in this room, is get out there and talk about SDI. Explain it, debate it, tell the American people the facts. It may well be the most important work we do in the next few years. And if we try, we'll succeed. So, we have great work ahead of us, big work. But if we do it together and with complete commitment, we can change our country and history forever.

Once during the campaign, I said, "This is a wonderful time to be alive," and I meant that. I meant that we're lucky not to live in pale and timid times. We've been blessed with the opportunity to stand for something-for liberty and freedom and fairness. And these are things worth fighting for, worth devoting our lives to. And we have good reason to be hopeful and optimistic.

We've made much progress already. So, let us go forth with good cheer and stout hearts – happy warriors out to seize back a country and a world to freedom.

Thank you, and God bless you. Thank you very much.

Tear Down This Wall

On June 12, 1987, Reagan spoke at the Brandenburg Gate in West Berlin with the Berlin Wall as his backdrop. His speech was also audible on the East Berlin side of the wall.

Chancellor Kohl, Governing Mayor Diepgen, ladies and gentlemen: Twenty-four years ago, President John F. Kennedy visited Berlin, speaking to the people of this city and the world at the City Hall. Well, since then two other presidents have come, each in his turn, to Berlin. And today I, myself, make my second visit to your city.

We come to Berlin, we American presidents, because it's our duty to speak, in this place, of freedom. But I must confess, we're drawn here by other things as well: by the feeling of history in this city, more than 500 years older than our own nation; by the beauty of the Grunewald and the Tiergarten; most of all, by your courage and determination. Perhaps the composer Paul Lincke understood something about American presidents. You see, like so many presidents before me, I come here today because wherever I go, whatever I do: *Ich hab noch einen Koffer in Berlin.* [I still have a suitcase in Berlin.]

Our gathering today is being broadcast throughout Western Europe and North America. I understand that it is being seen and heard as well in the East. To those listening throughout Eastern Europe, a special word: Although I cannot be with you, I address my remarks to you just as surely as to those standing here before me. For I join you, as I join your fellow countrymen in the West, in this firm, this unalterable belief: *Es gibt nur ein Berlin.* [There is only one Berlin.]

Behind me stands a wall that encircles the free sectors of this city, part of a vast system of barriers that divides the entire continent of Europe. From the Baltic, south, those barriers cut across Germany in a gash of barbed wire, concrete, dog runs, and guard towers. Farther south, there may be no visible, no obvious wall. But there remain armed guards and checkpoints all the same—still a restriction on the right to travel, still an instrument to impose upon ordinary men and women the will of a totalitarian state. Yet it is here in Berlin where the wall emerges most clearly; here, cutting across your city, where the news photo and the television screen have imprinted this brutal division of a continent upon the mind of the world. Standing before the Brandenburg Gate, every man is a German, separated from his fellow men. Every man is a Berliner, forced to look upon a scar.

President von Weizsacker has said, "The German question is open as long as the Brandenburg Gate is closed." Today I say: As long as the gate is closed, as long as this scar of a wall is permitted to stand, it is not the German question alone that remains open, but the question of freedom for all mankind. Yet I do not come here to lament. For I find in Berlin a message of hope, even in the shadow of this wall, a message of triumph.

In this season of spring in 1945, the people of Berlin emerged from their air-raid shelters to find devastation. Thousands of miles away, the people of the United States reached out to help. And in 1947 Secretary of State—as you've been told—George Marshall announced the creation of what would become known as the Marshall Plan. Speaking precisely 40 years ago this month, he said: "Our policy is directed not against any country or doctrine, but against hunger, poverty, desperation, and chaos."

In the Reichstag a few moments ago, I saw a display commemorating this 40th anniversary of the Marshall Plan. I was struck by the sign on a burnt-out, gutted structure that was being rebuilt. I understand that Berliners of my own generation can remember seeing signs like it dotted throughout the western sectors of the city. The sign read simply: "The Marshall Plan is helping here to strengthen the free world." A strong, free world in the West, that dream became real. Japan rose from ruin to become an economic giant. Italy, France, Belgium—virtually every nation in Western Europe saw political and economic rebirth; the European Community was founded.

In West Germany and here in Berlin, there took place an economic miracle, the Wirtschaftswunder. Adenauer, Erhard, Reuter, and other leaders understood the practical importance of liberty—that just as truth can flourish only when the journalist is given freedom of speech, so prosperity can come about only when the farmer and businessman enjoy economic freedom. The German leaders reduced tariffs, expanded free trade, lowered taxes. From 1950 to 1960 alone, the standard of living in West Germany and Berlin doubled.

Where four decades ago there was rubble, today in West Berlin there is the greatest industrial output of any city in Germany—busy office blocks, fine homes and apartments, proud avenues, and the spreading lawns of parkland. Where a city's culture seemed to have been destroyed, today there are two great universities, orchestras and an opera, countless theaters, and museums. Where there was want, today there's abundance—food, clothing, automobiles—the wonderful goods of the Ku'damm. From devastation, from utter ruin, you Berliners have, in freedom, rebuilt a city that once again ranks as one of the greatest on earth. The Soviets may have had other plans. But my friends, there were a few things the Soviets didn't count on – *Berliner Herz, Berliner Humor, ja, und Berliner Schnauze.* [Berliner heart, Berliner humor, yes, and a Berliner Schnauze.]

In the 1950s, Khrushchev predicted: "We will bury you." But in the West today, we see a free world that has achieved a level of prosperity and well-being unprecedented in all human history. In the Communist world, we see failure, technological backwardness, declining standards of health, even want of the most basic kind—too little food. Even today, the Soviet Union still cannot feed itself. After these four decades, then, there stands before the entire world one great and inescapable conclusion: Freedom leads to prosperity. Freedom replaces the ancient hatreds among the nations with comity and peace. Freedom is the victor.

And now the Soviets themselves may, in a limited way, be coming to understand the importance of freedom. We hear much from Moscow about a new policy of reform and openness. Some political prisoners have been released. Certain foreign news broadcasts are no longer being jammed. Some economic enterprises have been permitted to operate with greater freedom from state control.

Are these the beginnings of profound changes in the Soviet state? Or are they token gestures, intended to raise false hopes in the West, or to strengthen the Soviet system without changing it? We welcome change and openness; for we believe that freedom and security go together, that the advance of human liberty can only strengthen the cause of world peace. There is one sign the Soviets can make that would be unmistakable, that would advance dramatically the cause of freedom and peace.

General Secretary Gorbachev, if you seek peace, if you seek prosperity for the Soviet Union and Eastern Europe, if you seek liberalization: Come here to this gate! Mr. Gorbachev, open this gate! Mr. Gorbachev, tear down this wall!

I understand the fear of war and the pain of division that afflict this continent—and I pledge to you my country's efforts to help overcome these burdens. To be sure, we in the West must resist Soviet expansion. So we must maintain defenses of unassailable strength. Yet we seek peace; so we must strive to reduce arms on both sides.

Beginning 10 years ago, the Soviets challenged the Western alliance with a grave new threat, hundreds of new and more deadly SS-20 nuclear missiles, capable of striking every capital in Europe. The Western alliance responded by committing itself to a counter-deployment unless the Soviets agreed to negotiate a better solution; namely, the elimination of such weapons on both sides. For many months, the Soviets refused to bargain in earnestness. As the alliance, in turn, prepared to go forward with its counter-deployment, there were difficult days—days of protests like those during my 1982 visit to this city—and the Soviets later walked away from the table.

But through it all, the alliance held firm. And I invite those who protested then— I invite those who protest today—to mark this fact: Because we remained strong, the Soviets came back to the table. And because we remained strong, today we have within reach the possibility, not merely of limiting the growth of arms, but of eliminating, for the first time, an entire class of nuclear weapons from the face of the earth.

As I speak, NATO ministers are meeting in Iceland to review the progress of our proposals for eliminating these weapons. At the talks in Geneva, we have also proposed deep cuts in strategic offensive weapons. And the Western allies have likewise made far-reaching proposals to reduce the danger of conventional war and to place a total ban on chemical weapons.

While we pursue these arms reductions, I pledge to you that we will maintain the capacity to deter Soviet aggression at any level at which it might occur. And in cooperation with many of our allies, the United States is pursuing the Strategic Defense Initiative—research to base deterrence not on the threat of offensive retaliation, but on defenses that truly defend; on systems, in short, that will not target populations, but shield them. By these means we seek to increase the safety of Europe and all the world. But we must remember a crucial fact: East and West do not mistrust each other because we are armed; we are armed because we mistrust each other. And our differences are not about weapons but about liberty. When President Kennedy spoke at the City Hall those 24 years ago, freedom was encircled, Berlin was under siege. And today, despite all the pressures upon this city, Berlin stands secure in its liberty. And freedom itself is transforming the globe.

In the Philippines, in South and Central America, democracy has been given a rebirth. Throughout the Pacific, free markets are working miracle after miracle of economic growth. In the industrialized nations, a technological revolution is taking place—a revolution marked by rapid, dramatic advances in computers and telecommunications.

In Europe, only one nation and those it controls refuse to join the community of freedom. Yet in this age of redoubled economic growth, of information and innovation, the Soviet Union faces a choice: It must make fundamental changes, or it will become obsolete.

Today thus represents a moment of hope. We in the West stand ready to cooperate with the East to promote true openness, to break down barriers that separate people, to create a safe, freer world. And surely there is no better place than Berlin, the meeting place of East and West, to make a start. Free people of Berlin: Today, as in the past, the United States stands for the strict observance and full implementation of all parts of the Four Power Agreement of 1971. Let us use this occasion, the 750th anniversary of this city, to usher in a new era, to seek a still fuller, richer life for the Berlin of the future. Together, let us maintain and develop the ties between the Federal Republic and the Western sectors of Berlin, which is permitted by the 1971 agreement.

And I invite Mr. Gorbachev: Let us work to bring the Eastern and Western parts of the city closer together, so that all the inhabitants of all Berlin can enjoy the benefits that come with life in one of the great cities of the world.

To open Berlin still further to all Europe, East and West, let us expand the vital air access to this city, finding ways of making commercial air service to Berlin more convenient, more comfortable, and more economical. We look to the day when West Berlin can become one of the chief aviation hubs in all central Europe.

With our French and British partners, the United States is prepared to help bring international meetings to Berlin. It would be only fitting for Berlin to serve as the site of United Nations meetings, or world conferences on human rights and arms control or other issues that call for international cooperation.

There is no better way to establish hope for the future than to enlighten young minds, and we would be honored to sponsor summer youth exchanges, cultural events, and other programs for young Berliners from the East. Our French and British friends, I'm certain, will do the same. And it's my hope that an authority can be found in East Berlin to sponsor visits from young people of the Western sectors.

One final proposal, one close to my heart: Sport represents a source of enjoyment and ennoblement, and you may have noted that the Republic of Korea—South Korea—has offered to permit certain events of the 1988 Olympics to take place in the North. International sports competitions of all kinds could take place in both parts of this city. And what better way to demonstrate to the world the openness of this city than to offer in some future year to hold the Olympic games here in Berlin, East and West? In these four decades, as I have said, you Berliners have built a great city. You've done so in spite of threats–the Soviet attempts to impose the East-mark, the blockade. Today the city thrives in spite of the challenges implicit in the very presence of this wall. What keeps you here? Certainly there's a great deal to be said for your fortitude, for your defiant courage. But I believe there's something deeper, something that involves Berlin's whole look and feel and way of life–not mere sentiment. No one could live long in Berlin without being completely disabused of illusions. Something instead, that has seen the difficulties of life in Berlin but chose to accept them, that continues to build this good and proud city in contrast to a surrounding totalitarian presence that refuses to release human energies or aspirations. Something that speaks with a powerful voice of affirmation, that says yes to this city, yes to the future, yes to freedom. In a word, I would submit that what keeps you in Berlin is love–love both profound and abiding.

Perhaps this gets to the root of the matter, to the most fundamental distinction of all between East and West. The totalitarian world produces backwardness because it does such violence to the spirit, thwarting the human impulse to create, to enjoy, to worship. The totalitarian world finds even symbols of love and of worship an affront. Years ago, before the East Germans began rebuilding their churches, they erected a secular structure: the television tower at Alexander Platz. Virtually ever since, the authorities have been working to correct what they view as the tower's one major flaw, treating the glass sphere at the top with paints and chemicals of every kind. Yet even today when the sun strikes that sphere–that sphere that towers over all Berlin–the light makes the sign of the cross. There in Berlin, like the city itself, symbols of love, symbols of worship, cannot be suppressed.

As I looked out a moment ago from the Reichstag, that embodiment of German unity, I noticed words crudely spray-painted upon the wall, perhaps by a young Berliner: "This wall will fall. Beliefs become reality." Yes, across Europe, this wall will fall. For it cannot withstand faith; it cannot withstand truth. The wall cannot withstand freedom.

And I would like, before I close, to say one word. I have read, and I have been questioned since I've been here about certain demonstrations against my coming. And I would like to say just one thing, and to those who demonstrate so. I wonder if they have ever asked themselves that if they should have the kind of government they apparently seek, no one would ever be able to do what they're doing again.

Thank you and God bless you all.

To the Students of Moscow State University

Among the breath-taking events of the end of the Cold War was a speech, given by President Reagan before an audience of students at Moscow State University on May 31, 1988. This is a condensed version of that speech.

Before I left Washington, I received many heartfelt letters and telegrams asking me to carry here a simple message - perhaps, but also some of the most important business of this summit - it is a message of peace and goodwill and hope for a growing friendship and closeness between our two peoples.

First I want to take a little time to talk to you much as I would to any group of university students in the United States. I want to talk not just of the realities of today, but of the possibilities of tomorrow.

You know, one of the first contacts between your country and mine took place between Russian and American explorers. The Americans were members of Cook's last voyage on an expedition searching for an Arctic passage; on the island of Unalaska, they came upon the Russians, who took them in, and together, with the native inhabitants, held a prayer service on the ice.

The explorers of the modern era are the entrepreneurs, men with vision, with the courage to take risks and faith enough to brave the unknown. These entrepreneurs and their small enterprises are responsible for almost all the economic growth in the United States. They are the prime movers of the technological revolution. In fact, one of the largest personal computer firms in the United states was started by two college students, no older than you, in the garage behind their home.

Some people, even in my own country, look at the riot of experiment that is the free market and see only waste. What of all the entrepreneurs that fail? Well, many do, particularly the successful ones. Often several times. And if you ask them the secret of their success, they'll tell you, it's all that they learned in their struggles along the way - yes, it's what they learned from failing. Like an athlete in competition, or a scholar in pursuit of the truth, experience is the greatest teacher.

We are seeing the power of economic freedom spreading around the world - places such as the Republic of Korea, Singapore, and Taiwan have vaulted into the technological era, barely pausing in the industrial age along the way. Low-tax agricultural policies in the sub-continent mean that in some years India is now a net exporter of food. Perhaps most exciting are the winds of change that are blowing over the People's republic of China, where one-quarter of the world's population is now getting its first taste of economic freedom.

At the same time, the growth of democracy has become one of the most powerful political movements of our age. In Latin America in the 1970's, only a third of the population lived under democratic government. Today over 90 percent does. In the Philippines, in the Republic of Korea, free, contested, democratic elections are the order of the day. Throughout the world, free markets are the model for growth. Democracy is the standard by which governments are measured.

We Americans make no secret of our belief in freedom. In fact, it's something of a national pastime. Every four years the American people choose a new president, and 1988 is one of those years. At one point there were 13 major candidates running in the two major parties, not to mention all the others, including the Socialist and Libertarian candidates - all trying to get my job.

About 1,000 local television stations, 8,500 radio stations, and 1,700 daily newspapers, each one an independent, private enterprise, fiercely independent of the government, report on the candidates, grill them in interviews, and bring them together for debates. In the end, the people vote - they decide who will be the next president.

But freedom doesn't begin or end with elections. Go to any American town, to take just an example, and you'll see dozens of synagogues and mosques - and you'll see families of every conceivable nationality, worshipping together.

Go into any schoolroom, and there you will see children being taught the Declaration of Independence, that they are endowed by their Creator with certain unalienable rights - among them life, liberty, and the pursuit of happiness - that no government can justly deny - the guarantees in their Constitution for freedom of speech, freedom of assembly, and freedom of religion.

Go into any courtroom and there will preside an independent judge, beholden to no government power. There every defendant has the right to a trial by a jury of his peers, usually 12 men and women - common citizens, they are the ones, the only ones, who weigh the evidence and decide on guilt or innocence. In that court, the accused is innocent until proven guilty, and the word of a policeman, or any official, has no greater legal standing than the word of the accused.

Go to any university campus, and there you'll find an open, sometimes heated discussion of the problems in American society and what can be done to correct them. Turn on the television, and you'll see the legislature conducting the business of government right there before the camera, debating and voting on the legislation that will become the law of the land. March in any demonstrations, and there are many of them - the people's right of assembly is guaranteed in the Constitution and protected by the police.

But freedom is more even than this: Freedom is the right to question, and change the established way of doing things. It is the continuing revolution of the marketplace. It is the understanding that allows us to recognize shortcomings and seek solutions. It is the right to put forth an idea, scoffed at by the experts, and watch it catch fire among the people. It is the right to stick - to dream - to follow your dream, or stick to your conscience, even if you're the only one in a sea of doubters.

Freedom is the recognition that no single person, no single authority of government has a monopoly on the truth, but that every individual life is infinitely precious, that every one of us put on this world has been put there for a reason and has something to offer.

America is a nation made up of hundreds of nationalities. Our ties to you are more than ones of good feeling; they're ties of kinship. In America, you'll find Russians, Armenians, Ukrainians, peoples from Eastern Europe and Central Asia. They come from every part of this vast continent, from every continent, to live in harmony, seeking a place where each cultural heritage is respected, each is valued for its diverse strengths and beauties and the richness it brings to our lives.

Recently, a few individuals and families have been allowed to visit relatives in the West. We can only hope that it won't be long before all are allowed to do so, and Ukrainian-Americans, Baltic-Americans, Armenian-Americans, can freely visit their homelands, just as this Irish-American visits his.

Freedom, it has been said, makes people selfish and materialistic, but Americans are one of the most religious peoples on Earth. Because they know that liberty, just as life itself, is not earned, but a gift from God, they seek to share that gift with the world. "Reason and experience," said George Washington, in his farewell address, "both forbid us to expect that national morality can prevail in exclusion of religious principle. And it is substantially true, that virtue or morality is a necessary spring of popular government."

Democracy is less a system of government than it is a system to keep government limited, unintrusive: A system of constraints on power to keep politics and government secondary to the important things in life, the true sources of value found only in family and faith.

I have often said, nations do not distrust each other because they are armed; they are armed because they distrust each other. If this globe is to live in peace and prosper, if it is to embrace all the possibilities of the technological revolution, then nations must renounce, once and for all, the right to an expansionist foreign policy. Peace between nations must be an enduring goal - not a tactical stage in a continuing conflict.

I've been told that there's a popular song in your country - perhaps you know it - whose evocative refrain asks the question, "Do the Russians want a war?" In answer it says, "Go ask that silence lingering in the air, above the birch and poplar there; beneath those trees the soldiers lie. Go ask my mother, ask my wife; then you will have to ask no more, 'Do the Russians want a war?'"

But what of your one-time allies? What of those who embraced you on the Elbe? What if we were to ask the watery graves of the Pacific, or the European battlefields where America's fallen were buried far from home? What if we were to ask their mothers, sisters, and sons, do Americans want war? Ask us, too, and you'll find the same answer, the same longing in every heart. People do not make wars, governments do - and no mother would ever willingly sacrifice her sons for territorial gain, for economic advantage, for ideology. A people free to choose will always choose peace.

Americans seek always to make friends of old antagonists. After a colonial revolution with Britain we have cemented for all ages the ties of kinship between our nations. After a terrible civil war between North and South, we healed our wounds and found true unity as a nation. We fought two world wars in my lifetime against Germany and one with Japan, but now the Federal Republic of Germany and Japan are two of our closest allies and friends.

Some people point to the trade disputes between us as a sign of strain, but they're the frictions of all families, and the family of free nations is a big and vital and sometimes boisterous one. I can tell you that nothing would please my heart more than in my lifetime to see American and Soviet diplomats grappling with the problem of trade disputes between America and a growing, exuberant, exporting Soviet Union that had opened up to economic freedom and growth.

Is this just a dream? Perhaps. But it is a dream that is our responsibility to have come true.

Your generation is living in one of the most exciting, hopeful times in Soviet history. It is a time when the first breath of freedom stirs the air and the heart beats to the accelerated rhythm of hope, when the accumulated spiritual energies of a long silence yearn to break free.

We do not know what the conclusion of this journey will be, but we're hopeful that the promise of reform will be fulfilled. In this Moscow spring, this May 1988, we may be allowed that hope - that freedom, like the fresh green sapling planted over Tolstoi's grave, will blossom forth at least in the rich fertile soil of your people and culture. We may be allowed to hope that the marvelous sound of a new openness will keep rising through, ringing through, leading to a new world of reconciliation, friendship, and peace.

Thank you all very much and *da blagoslovit vas gospod!* God bless you.

Farewell Address

Ronald Reagan offered a formal farewell to the nation in this January 11, 1989, address from the Oval Office of the White House as he neared the end of two terms in office.

This is the 34th time I'll speak to you from the Oval Office and the last. We've been together eight years now, and soon it'll be time for me to go. But before I do, I wanted to share some thoughts, some of which I've been saving for a long time.

It's been the honor of my life to be your president. So many of you have written the past few weeks to say thanks, but I could say as much to you. Nancy and I are grateful for the opportunity you gave us to serve.

One of the things about the presidency is that you're always somewhat apart. You spend a lot of time going by too fast in a car someone else is driving, and seeing the people through tinted glass–the parents holding up a child, and the wave you saw too late and couldn't return. And so many times I wanted to stop and reach out from behind the glass, and connect. Well, maybe I can do a little of that tonight.

People ask how I feel about leaving. And the fact is, "parting is such sweet sorrow." The sweet part is California, and the ranch and freedom. The sorrow–the goodbyes, of course, and leaving this beautiful place.

You know, down the hall and up the stairs from this office is the part of the White House where the president and his family live. There are a few favorite windows I have up there that I like to stand and look out of early in the morning. The view is over the grounds here to the Washington Monument, and then the Mall and the Jefferson Memorial. But on mornings when the humidity is low, you can see past the Jefferson to the river, the Potomac, and the Virginia shore. Someone said that's the view Lincoln had when he saw the smoke rising from the Battle of Bull Run. I see more prosaic things: the grass on the banks, the morning traffic as people make their way to work, now and then a sailboat on the river.

I've been thinking a bit at that window. I've been reflecting on what the past eight years have meant and mean. And the image that comes to mind like a refrain is a nautical one–a small story about a big ship, and a refugee and a sailor. It was back in the early '80s, at the height of the boat people. And the sailor was hard at work on the carrier Midway, which was patrolling the South China Sea. The sailor, like most American servicemen, was young, smart, and fiercely observant. The crew spied on the horizon a leaky little boat. And crammed inside were refugees from Indochina hoping to get to America. The Midway sent a small launch to bring them to the ship and safety. As the refugees made their way through the choppy seas, one spied the sailor on deck and stood up and called out to him. He yelled, "Hello, American sailor. Hello, freedom man."

A small moment with a big meaning, a moment the sailor, who wrote it in a letter, couldn't get out of his mind. And when I saw it, neither could I. Because that's what it was to be an American in the 1980s. We stood, again, for freedom. I know we always have, but in the past few years the world again, and in a way, we ourselves rediscovered it.

It's been quite a journey this decade, and we held together through some stormy seas. And at the end, together, we are reaching our destination.

The fact is, from Grenada to the Washington and Moscow summits, from the recession of '81 to '82, to the expansion that began in late '82 and continues to this day, we've made a difference. The way I see it, there were two great triumphs, two things that I'm proudest of. One is the economic recovery, in which the people of America created—and filled—19 million new jobs. The other is the recovery of our morale. America is respected again in the world and looked to for leadership.

Something that happened to me a few years ago reflects some of this. It was back in 1981, and I was attending my first big economic summit, which was held that year in Canada. The meeting place rotates among the member countries. The opening meeting was a formal dinner for the heads of government of the seven industrialized nations. Now, I sat there like the new kid in school and listened, and it was all Francois this and Helmut that. They dropped titles and spoke to one another on a first-name basis. Well, at one point I sort of leaned in and said, "My name's Ron." Well, in that same year, we began the actions we felt would ignite an economic comeback—cut taxes and regulation, started to cut spending. And soon the recovery began.

Two years later another economic summit, with pretty much the same cast. At the big opening meeting we all got together, and all of a sudden, just for a moment, I saw that everyone was just sitting there looking at me. And one of them broke the silence. "Tell us about the American miracle," he said.

Well, back in 1980, when I was running for president, it was all so different. Some pundits said our programs would result in catastrophe.

Our views on foreign affairs would cause war. Our plans for the economy would cause inflation to soar and bring about economic collapse. I even remember one highly respected economist saying, back in 1982, that "the engines of economic growth have shut down here, and they're likely to stay that way for years to come." Well, he and the other opinion leaders were wrong. The fact is, what they called "radical" was really "right." What they called "dangerous" was just "desperately needed."

And in all of that time I won a nickname, "The Great Communicator." But I never thought it was my style or the words I used that made a difference: It was the content. I wasn't a great communicator, but I communicated great things, and they didn't spring full bloom from my brow, they came from the heart of a great nation—from our experience, our wisdom, and our belief in principles that have guided us for two centuries. They called it the Reagan revolution. Well, I'll accept that, but for me it always seemed more like the great rediscovery, a rediscovery of our values and our common sense.

Common sense told us that when you put a big tax on something, the people will produce less of it. So, we cut the people's tax rates, and the people produced more than ever before. The economy bloomed like a plant that had been cut back and could now grow quicker and stronger. Our economic program brought about the longest peacetime expansion in our history: real family income up, the poverty rate down, entrepreneurship booming, and an explosion in research and new technology. We're exporting more than ever because American industry became more competitive and at the same time, we summoned the national will to knock down protectionist walls abroad instead of erecting them at home. Common sense also told us that to preserve the peace, we'd have to become strong again after years of weakness and confusion. So, we rebuilt our defenses, and this New Year we toasted the new peacefulness around the globe. Not only have the superpowers actually begun to reduce their stockpiles of nuclear weapons—and hope for even more progress is bright—but the regional conflicts that rack the globe are also beginning to cease. The Persian Gulf is no longer a war zone. The Soviets are leaving Afghanistan. The Vietnamese are preparing to pull out of Cambodia, and an American-mediated accord will soon send 50,000 Cuban troops home from Angola.

The lesson of all this was, of course, that because we're a great nation, our challenges seem complex. It will always be this way. But as long as we remember our first principles and believe in ourselves, the future will always be ours. And something else we learned: Once you begin a great movement, there's no telling where it will end. We meant to change a nation, and instead, we changed a world.

Countries across the globe are turning to free markets and free speech and turning away from ideologies of the past. For them, the great rediscovery of the 1980s has been that, lo and behold, the moral way of government is the practical way of government: Democracy, the profoundly good, is also the profoundly productive.

When you've got to the point when you can celebrate the anniversaries of your 39th birthday, you can sit back sometimes, review your life, and see it flowing before you. For me there was a fork in the river, and it was right in the middle of my life. I never meant to go into politics. It wasn't my intention when I was young. But I was raised to believe you had to pay your way for the blessings bestowed on you. I was happy with my career in the entertainment world, but I ultimately went into politics because I wanted to protect something precious.

Ours was the first revolution in the history of mankind that truly reversed the course of government, and with three little words: "We the people." "We the people" tell the government what to do, it doesn't tell us. "We the people" are the driver, the government is the car. And we decide where it should go, and by what route, and how fast. Almost all the world's constitutions are documents in which governments tell the people what their privileges are. Our Constitution is a document in which "We the people" tell the government what it is allowed to do. "We the people" are free. This belief has been the underlying basis for everything I've tried to do these past eight years.

But back in the 1960s, when I began, it seemed to me that we'd begun reversing the order of things—that through more and more rules and regulations and confiscatory taxes, the government was taking more of our money, more of our options, and more of our freedom. I went into politics in part to put up my hand and say, "Stop." I was a citizen politician, and it seemed the right thing for a citizen to do.

I think we have stopped a lot of what needed stopping. And I hope we have once again reminded people that man is not free unless government is limited. There's a clear cause and effect here that is as neat and predictable as a law of physics: As government expands, liberty contracts.

Nothing is less free than pure communism, and yet we have, the past few years, forged a satisfying new closeness with the Soviet Union. I've been asked if this isn't a gamble, and my answer is no because we're basing our actions not on words but deeds. The detente of the 1970s was based not on actions but promises. They'd promise to treat their own people and the people of the world better. But the gulag was still the gulag, and the state was still expansionist, and they still waged proxy wars in Africa, Asia, and Latin America.

Well, this time, so far, it's different. President Gorbachev has brought about some internal democratic reforms and begun the withdrawal from Afghanistan. He has also freed prisoners whose names I've given him every time we've met.

But life has a way of reminding you of big things through small incidents. Once, during the heady days of the Moscow summit, Nancy and I decided to break off from the entourage one afternoon to visit the shops on Arbat Street–that's a little street just off Moscow's main shopping area. Even though our visit was a surprise, every Russian there immediately recognized us and called out our names and reached for our hands. We were just about swept away by the warmth. You could almost feel the possibilities in all that joy. But within seconds, a KGB detail pushed their way toward us and began pushing and shoving the people in the crowd. It was an interesting moment. It reminded me that while the man on the street in the Soviet Union yearns for peace, the government is Communist. And those who run it are Communists, and that means we and they view such issues as freedom and human rights very differently.

We must keep up our guard, but we must also continue to work together to lessen and eliminate tension and mistrust. My view is that President Gorbachev is different from previous Soviet leaders. I think he knows some of the things wrong with his society and is trying to fix them. We wish him well. And we'll continue to work to make sure that the Soviet Union that eventually emerges from this process is a less threatening one. What it all boils down to is this. I want the new closeness to continue. And it will, as long as we make it clear that we will continue to act in a certain way as long as they continue to act in a helpful manner. If and when they don't, at first pull your punches. If they persist, pull the plug. It's still trust but verify. It's still play, but cut the cards. It's still watch closely. And don't be afraid to see what you see.

I've been asked if I have any regrets. Well, I do. The deficit is one. I've been talking a great deal about that lately, but tonight isn't for arguments. And I'm going to hold my tongue. But an observation: I've had my share of victories in the Congress, but what few people noticed is that I never won anything you didn't win for me. They never saw my troops, they never saw Reagan's regiments, the American people. You won every battle with every call you made and letter you wrote demanding action. Well, action is still needed. If we're to finish the job, Reagan's regiments will have to become the Bush brigades. Soon he'll be the chief, and he'll need you every bit as much as I did. Finally, there is a great tradition of warnings in presidential farewells, and I've got one that's been on my mind for some time. But oddly enough it starts with one of the things I'm proudest of in the past eight years: the resurgence of national pride that I called the new patriotism. This national feeling is good, but it won't count for much, and it won't last unless it's grounded in thoughtfulness and knowledge.

An informed patriotism is what we want. And are we doing a good enough job teaching our children what America is and what she represents in the long history of the world? Those of us who are over 35 or so years of age grew up in a different America. We were taught, very directly, what it means to be an American. And we absorbed, almost in the air, a love of country and an appreciation of its institutions. If you didn't get these things from your family, you got them from the neighborhood, from the father down the street who fought in Korea or the family who lost someone at Anzio. Or you could get a sense of patriotism from school. And if all else failed, you could get a sense of patriotism from popular culture. The movies celebrated democratic values and implicitly reinforced the idea that America was special. TV was like that, too, through the mid-'60s

But now, we're about to enter the '90s, and some things have changed. Younger parents aren't sure that an unambivalent appreciation of America is the right thing to teach modern children. And as for those who create the popular culture, well-grounded patriotism is no longer the style. Our spirit is back, but we haven't reinstitutionalized it. We've got to do a better job of getting across that America is freedom—freedom of speech, freedom of religion, freedom of enterprise. And freedom is special and rare. It's fragile; it needs protection.

So, we've got to teach history based not on what's in fashion but what's important: Why the Pilgrims came here, who Jimmy Doolittle was, and what those 30 seconds over Tokyo meant. You know, four years ago on the 40th anniversary of D-Day, I read a letter from a young woman writing of her late father, who'd fought on Omaha Beach. Her name was Lisa Zanatta Henn, and she said, "We will always remember, we will never forget what the boys of Normandy did." Well, let's help her keep her word. If we forget what we did, we won't know who we are. I'm warning of an eradication of the American memory that could result, ultimately, in an erosion of the American spirit. Let's start with some basics: more attention to American history and a greater emphasis on civic ritual. And let me offer lesson No. 1 about America: All great change in America begins at the dinner table. So, tomorrow night in the kitchen I hope the talking begins. And children, if your parents haven't been teaching you what it means to be an American, let 'em know and nail 'em on it. That would be a very American thing to do.

And that's about all I have to say tonight. Except for one thing. The past few days when I've been at that window upstairs, I've thought a bit of the "shining city upon a hill." The phrase comes from John Winthrop, who wrote it to describe the America he imagined. What he imagined was important because he was an early Pilgrim, an early freedom man. He journeyed here on what today we'd call a little wooden boat; and like the other Pilgrims, he was looking for a home that would be free.

I've spoken of the shining city all my political life, but I don't know if I ever quite communicated what I saw when I said it. But in my mind it was a tall proud city built on rocks stronger than oceans, wind-swept, God-blessed, and teeming with people of all kinds living in harmony and peace, a city with free ports that hummed with commerce and creativity, and if there had to be city walls, the walls had doors and the doors were open to anyone with the will and the heart to get here. That's how I saw it and see it still.

And how stands the city on this winter night? More prosperous, more secure, and happier than it was eight years ago. But more than that; after 200 years, two centuries, she still stands strong and true on the granite ridge, and her glow has held steady no matter what storm. And she's still a beacon, still a magnet for all who must have freedom, for all the pilgrims from all the lost places who are hurtling through the darkness, toward home.

We've done our part. And as I walk off into the city streets, a final word to the men and women of the Reagan revolution, the men and women across America who for eight years did the work that brought America back. My friends: We did it. We weren't just marking time. We made a difference. We made the city stronger. We made the city freer, and we left her in good hands. All in all, not bad, not bad at all.

And so, good-bye, God bless you, and God bless the United States of America.

About the Authors

Brad Lips is the Chief Operating Officer of the Atlas Economic Research Foundation, which advances the international freedom movement by assisting startup think tanks and linking them to a global network of principled, independent research institutes.

Dan Lips is a Senior Fellow with the Goldwater Institute and a Policy Analyst at the Americans for Prosperity Foundation. Previously, Dan Lips was president of a non-profit organization working to advance school choice in Arizona.

Both Dan and Brad graduated from Princeton University and collaborate on the ReaganVision.com website. They can be reached at info@ReaganVision.com.

Este libro se terminó de imprimir en el mes de
Septiembre del 2004, en Editora Centenario S. A.
Av. Monumental No. 6, Cristo Redentor,
E-mail: editcentenario@codetel.net.do
Santo Domingo, República Dominicana